Phy… of the …paniel

(from The Kennel Club breed standard)

Tail: Set low, well feathered, carried level with back.

Hindquarters: Very powerful and well developed. Hocks low, stifles well bent and set straight.

Colour: Plain white body preferred, with lemon markings; orange permissible. Slight head markings and freckled muzzle.

Size: Ideal weight: dogs: 36 kgs (80 lbs); bitches: 29.5 kgs (65 lbs).

Coat: Abundant, close, silky and straight. Legs and chest well feathered.

Feet: Large, round, well covered with hair.

Clumber Spaniel

by Ricky Blackman

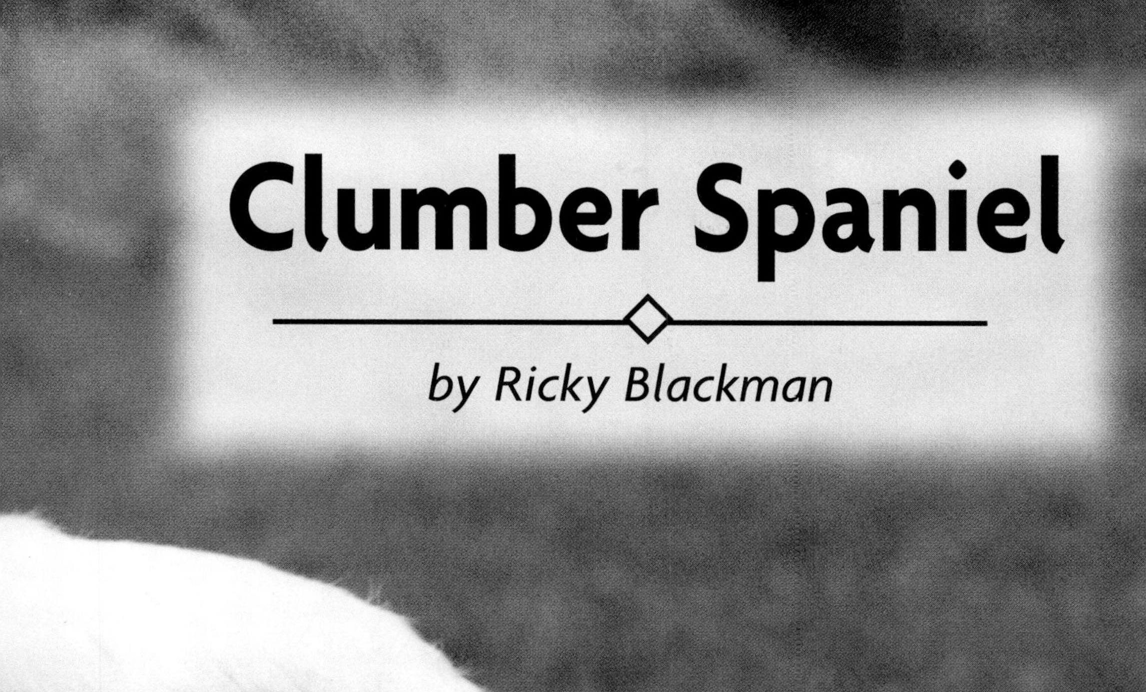

Table of Contents

PUBLISHED IN THE UNITED KINGDOM BY:

INTERPET PUBLISHING

Vincent Lane, Dorking
Surrey RH4 3YX
England

ISBN 1-902389-23-9

PHOTOGRAPHY BY MARY BLOOM

with additional photos by:
John L Ashbey
Robert F & Jane L Bonaccorso
Karin Brostam
Gail Budde
Sue Carr
Vicky and Warren Cook
Margaret Curtis
Leigh Ehrenkrantz
Walt and Jan Friis
Pat Fraser
Roe and Gordie Froman
Carol Ann Johnson
Barbara Stebbins

Illustrations by Renée Low

The author wishes to express special thanks to Roe Froman, DVM, for her excellent work on the health sections of this book. She was kind enough to share with us her particular knowledge as it applies to our breed. *Special thanks to the owners.

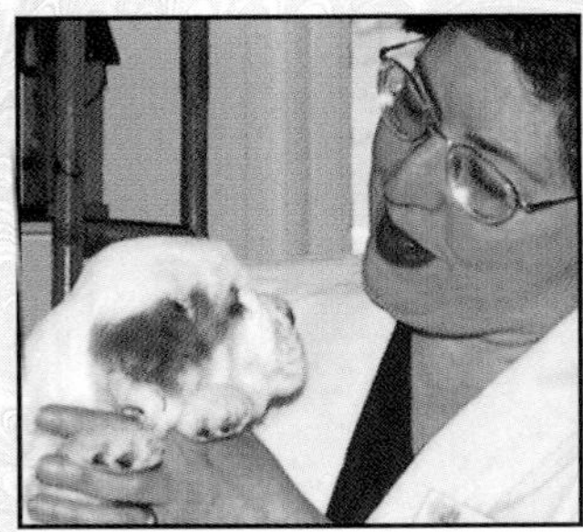

*The publisher thanks all of the owners of dogs in this book, especially Ricky Blackman, Sue Carr and Leigh Ehrenkrantz.

ANCESTRY OF THE CLUMBER SPANIEL

The Clumber Spaniel as a distinct breed has been a part of the English canine tradition since the 18th century. Early examples of dogs that looked like Clumber Spaniels have been unearthed in countries over the years, but no actual independent or co-existent strain was found in France or elsewhere on the Continent. Therefore, fanciers are faced with an intriguing mystery when trying to trace the Clumber Spaniel's actual origin. We do know that the name for the breed came from Clumber Park, the seat of the Duke of Newcastle in the late 18th century. As was the custom with nobles proud of their dogs, he or someone associated with the estate named the breed after his hereditary estate. Though the grand house burned down in 1938, one can still visit the grounds of Clumber Park (which is now part of the National Trust) and find the graves of some of the Clumbers who lived on the estate.

Though the Duke and his Clumber Spaniels shared the

Clumber Spaniels were bred as specialised hunters. This accomplished Clumber is Am and Can Ch Deke Slayton, showing off his exquisite nose.

property, he was probably not responsible for the breed's evolution, or at least there is no definite evidence of it. He is shown in an early painting with dogs that are early specimens of the Clumber Spaniel, but some think that these were the dogs that he was given. Students of the breed have advanced many theories about the origin of this unique dog, but concrete evidence for any one theory is lacking. This perhaps is all to the better—no one likes this kind of good mystery better than a dog lover, and especially a Clumber fancier! And so the debate rages on—people study old pictures, pore over old books for the faintest clues, write back and forth to England and France looking for evidence or pictures or details that everyone else has missed.

Here is a list of some of the better known theories regarding the origin of the breed along with the reasoning behind them:

1. The Clumber is French. Some believe that the breed developed in France and that the Duc de Noailles made a gift of all of his Clumbers to his friend the Duke of Newcastle in the latter part of the 18th century. According to tradition, this was done to save this excellent hunting dog from the perils of the French Revolution. This is the theory to which people subscribed faithfully for quite some time, but it has been rethought as no concrete evidence has been discovered to prove that the breed existed in France at such an early time.

2. The Clumber is English (first version). The English aristocracy has always had a great love of hunting. Good dogs were of paramount importance to the sport and the nobles staffed large kennels on their great estates to breed animals with specialised hunting functions. Several breeds were run in hunting packs and each performed a particular job, such as pointing, flushing and

This famous 19th-century paintings depicts the Clumber Spaniel as an excellent hunter and companion.

The great English artist, Gainsborough, painted Madame Lowndestone Norton. The small spaniel in the painting was known as a Clumber, though its resemblance to today's breed is minimal.

retrieving. In one such kennel—perhaps that of the Duke of Newcastle—an enterprising breeder/kennel manager may have crossed an English spaniel with a Basset Hound. What he got was a superior flushing dog with certain physical characteristics such as extended length and decreased height. Though fine animals such as this were jealously guarded by their owners, it is not unlikely that various noble families exchanged dogs, the interbreeding of which resulted in the very special large white Clumber.

An addendum to this theory is that the Clumber worked out so well in England that the dogs were given as highly prized gifts to the French aristocracy. New blood was possibly introduced into the line before they were sent back over to England during the French Revolution to reside at what is now considered to be the breed's ancestral home. Thus, we have a French contribution to this eminently English dog. This, of course, makes an especially romantic fairytale.

3. The Clumber is English (second version). In the beginning of this century, the well-known hunting and dog authority James Farrow wrote a monograph on the breed (the only book entirely on the breed until quite recently) and

DID YOU KNOW?

The first Clumber Spaniel to win the United States' prestigious Westminster Kennel Club dog show won that honour in 1996: Ch Clussexx Country Sunrise, owned by Richard and Judith Zaleski and professionally handled by Lisa Jane Alston-Myers. 'Brady', as he is known, won 13 all-breed Best in Show awards and is the breed's number-one sire in the US.

Ch Oakerland Repeater, owned by Miss M F Reed, is an early 20th-century Clumber Spaniel with a typical head but a relatively short body.

During the 1920s Clumbers were very variable in body length and height, as illustrated by Ch Sir Peter. Modern dogs have a completely different profile and a longer body.

In the early part of the 20th century, Miss Camilla Gurdon, daughter of Lady Cransworth, made a name for herself amongst Clumber Spaniel fanciers. This scene was photographed at Grundisburgh Hall, Suffolk.

theorised that the breed evolved from the larger Blenheim Spaniel. This was a solid hunting dog and also the ancestor of the present-day Cavalier King Charles Spaniel. He examined all of the theories then prevalent and felt that some dogs may have been exchanged as gifts between France and England but that this was originally an English breed.

4. The Clumber is Spanish. This theory purports that Clumbers were developed in Spain, gradually evolving from the heavy dog of Navarre into the hunting dog known as the Pachon, which is Spanish for phlegmatic. The Pachon was a calm and even-tempered hunting breed, some of which had a long, silky light-coloured coat. It is known that early in the 18th

The Clumber starts to take shape with its longer body. This 1890s photo shows a 60-pound dog named Lapis, bred by Mr W Arkwright, a leading authority on gundogs during the period.

At the beginning of the 20th century, a Clumber named Snow was considered to be an exceptionally fine specimen. Note how heavy the dog's body appears.

Rocketter was an outstanding Clumber at the end of the 19th century. He was bred by Messrs Holford, Foljambe and Arkwright. This photo is dated 1875.

The original Clumber is shown in this magnificent painting by Francis Wheatley in 1788. It depicts the Second Duke of Newcastle with the original type of Clumber Spaniel. These dogs were the gift of a French nobleman and took their name from the Duke's seat, Clumber Park, where this painting now hangs.

century numerous hunting dogs were imported to England from Spain, but unfortunately the trail goes cold and there is no record of the Pachon being part of those shipments. Enhancing the mystery is the fact that the word *spaniel* does refer to Spain as the origin of a strain of hunting dogs known as the Alpine Spaniel.

Whatever the origin, the Clumber Spaniel made its appearance in North America in 1844, first in Canada, and later in the United States. Prized mainly for their hunting ability and little known to the general public, Clumber Spaniels were shown in the early English shows starting in 1859. They were one of the first ten breeds recognised by the

DID YOU KNOW?

Dogs and wolves are members of the genus *Canis*. Wolves are known scientifically as *Canis lupus* while dogs are known as *Canis domesticus*. Dogs and wolves are known to interbreed. The term *canine* derives from the Latin derived word *Canis*. The term *dog* has no scientific basis but has been used for thousands of years. The origin of the word *dog* has never been authoritatively ascertained.

Am and Can Ch Smokerise Country Gentleman, owned by Margaret Curtis.

H M The King's Sandringham Spark. H M King George V, like his father H M King Edward VII, was a great believer in the Clumber Spaniel who had a formidable working dog kennel.

DID YOU KNOW?

Since dogs have been inbred for centuries, their physical and mental characteristics are constantly being

changed to suit man's desires for hunting, retrieving, scenting, guarding and warming their master's laps. During the past 150 years, dogs have been judged according to physical characteristics as well as functional abilities. Few breeds can boast a genuine balance between physique, working ability and temperament.

American Kennel Club in 1884 and began to appear in American rings in the early part of the 20th century. It has not been until the last 25 years that their popularity truly has moved in a positive direction.

Yes, Clumbers can retrieve, too. Here's Am and Can Ch Jetset's Deke Slayton, bringing home the pheasant.

CHARACTERISTICS OF THE CLUMBER SPANIEL

It is often heard that one breed or another is 'not for everyone.' Fortunately, there are over 300 breeds recognised by the Fédération Cynologique Internationale so that with proper study a prospective buyer can determine which one is best for him and his own particular living situation. Whilst it is true that every breed has its own individual characteristics, the buyer must know his own characteristics and needs to find what he is looking for in his new companion.

PERSONALITY

Clumber Spaniels are 'doggy' dogs. This means that they are 'in your face' dogs who do not lie in the corner all day and let the world go by. They possess some qualities that may not be desirable for every household. It is important to know what these are before you buy the dog. It is better for a breeder to let the prospective buyers know about the 'bad' or less desirable qualities first. In the Clumber, these qualities include casting coat, wet mouths and drooling, back problems and dirtier paws than most dogs.

Casting coat can be controlled with frequent brushing, and although a Clumber can get wet and muddy and appear to have brown feet, by the time he is dry most of the dirt will have fallen off and he will not even need a bath. However, if a completely neat, hairless house with light rugs or dark furniture is important to you, a Clumber Spaniel is not for you.

This breed, above all, is entertaining. Hardly a moment goes by without some antic, and a Clumber is very upset if this antic is not observed by someone and

Clumber Spaniels are loving, affectionate dogs. Are you ready to accept the love of a 'doggy' dog?

appreciated. Clumbers are loveable, and want to express their love every chance they get by kissing you or leaning on you or even attempting to sit on your lap. You can seldom forget there is a Clumber in the room. They snore, but they sleep in such fanciful positions that you laugh when you want to tell them to

Clumbers make handsome and cooperative models. The breed has continued to attract artists through the ages.

wake up and stop snoring. Clumbers are people lovers and sometimes can be overly enthusiastic about greetings, jumping up and wanting to be noticed. Although some would say that dogs cannot feel disappointment or emotions of that kind, if someone walks into a room and

Clumbers at home. Unfortunately many of them snore but they are so lovable that this minor shortcoming is happily overlooked.

does not pay attention to the Clumber, that dog is upset and cannot understand why he is being ignored. It is also a breed characteristic that when they are happy, possibly on just meeting you, they curve their bodies into almost a 'U' and wiggle around. Not every Clumber does this, but when you see it, it is charming and you will remember it.

Another characteristic of many Clumbers probably relates to their hunting background. A playful dog may exhibit its joy by picking up the nearest piece of clothing, a towel or another item and carrying it around. This can continue for quite some time; the dog does not chew or destroy his prize but simply wants his owner to appreciate his cuteness. Some

All Clumbers are different. By and large, the breed is trainable and enthusiastic, though some representatives tend to be stubborn, lazy and difficult to motivate.

Clumber Spaniels make excellent retrieving dogs, especially for bird work. This young Clumber is growing into a top-notch hunting dog.

will not even go outside unless they have something in their mouths.

It is hard to adequately describe the enthusiasm these dogs have for life and the simple pleasure they bring to their owners. A Clumber's tail will wag every time his owner enters the room as if his owner's presence itself were a gift to the dog. Perhaps this simply is the nature of the dog as a species that being partners with humans is his ultimate reason for being.

Clumbers are often homebodies who tend to be somewhat lazy. They enjoy sleeping on furniture more than anything else. Whilst they do like to cuddle up, they can be very active and like to play ball, take walks and run around with other dogs and children.

This breed can be taught most commands but will often pretend not to hear ones that conflict with its activity (or inactivity) of the moment. Good training practices will work well with Clumbers as with most breeds, but you will sometimes have to work harder at it.

Most Clumbers would not be described as athletic, but the soundness of the breed has improved greatly in the last twenty years. Although they like to spend a lot of time on the sofa, Clumbers will run and play in your fenced garden. They can also do obedience, track enthusiastically and perform their original purpose as hunting dogs in the field. In order to keep your dog slim and healthy, whether it is a pet or show dog, he must be exercised. This breed is a good all-purpose animal, but is happiest with his owner or another human, so long as he is paying attention to him. Walking and playing with the Clumber are good forms of exercise that also allow the owner to spend quality time with the dog.

Walking three (well-trained) Clumbers is a pleasure. Owners must devote at least an hour every day to give the Clumber his daily exercise.

Young Clumbers are easily trained to handle the bird with a soft mouth and return it to you. This puppy grew up to become an American and Canadian champion.

Clumbers love children and can tolerate a good deal of misconduct from a loving child. This child is having no luck lead-training his Clumber chum.

Clumber Spaniels were used as hunting dogs on great estates in the 18th and 19th centuries. The dogs were used with other breeds and each breed had its purpose. The Clumber's original function was as a flushing spaniel. His job was to get the bird into the air, after another breed had pointed to the bird's location. Still another breed would retrieve the birds after they were shot, although a Clumber can actually pick up a bird and bring it back quite well. There is a dedicated group of Clumber fanciers who still train their dogs for hunting, and it is hard to tell who enjoys it the most—the dog or the owner!

Whilst most Clumber owners would not feel that the breed can be described as a watchdog, Clumbers will often bark to announce a stranger or a squirrel approaching the house. Even their bark is not annoying, as they sound like they are barking with their mouth closed. However, it is most likely that the same dog will welcome that same human visitor into the house with wiggles of pleasure and nudging requests to be petted. A Clumber is not a barking dog and will seldom do so without a reason. The timbre of his bark is lower than most dogs, not ear piercing at all and will seem unusual the first time you hear it.

Socialisation is as important for this breed as any other, and the owner should ensure that the dog meets new people and enjoys new experiences. A dog should be part of the family and take part in as many activities as possible, either at home or away. One of the best ways for dogs to meet new

The author and her Clumbers, taking a break after exercise on the beach.

people is to walk about the centre of town or any other well-populated place. Usually a puppy will attract attention, and a Clumber even more so. Some Clumber puppies will urinate a little bit in their excitement, even at home. This small problem will go away as they get older.

PHYSICAL CHARACTERISTICS

The first impression of a Clumber is that it is heavier than you expected. Its long white hair reminds most people of a short white St. Bernard. Its heavy head and somewhat serious expression belie its outgoing and exuberant personality. It is a true spaniel with long, hairy ears, a full ruff, feathers (long hair) on its front legs and above its hocks and often a flag (long hairs) on its tail. Depending on the country, the tail may be docked or undocked. In many European countries it is unlawful now to dock the tail. In the United States there is a movement to change the standard to underline the fact that in the show ring a docked or undocked tail is of equal value. The breed should have heavy bone, and because of this the dogs weigh more than they appear to. The

Clumbers are gregarious dogs that get on well with cats and other dogs, if they are properly socialised.

An exuberant and outgoing personality characterises the smiling Clumber Spaniel.

Clumbers thrive on multiple hugs, especially from favourite children.

Clumber is considered a long dog, the height to length proportion being 9 to 11. This breed differs in shape considerably from other spaniels, such as the Springer. Specimens of this breed can be very good movers, but most have what is known as the 'Clumber roll,' in which the middle of the back swings somewhat from side to side. This is a breed characteristic and should not throw the dog off its actual movement. It should also not be confused with the roll of an overweight dog. According to the breed standard, a Clumber's particular gait is 'comfortable and can be maintained at a steady trot for a day of work in the fields without exhaustion.'

Clumber puppies are generally easygoing dogs, subject to bursts of enthusiasm and quiet times for contemplation and napping.

OWNER SUITABILITY

What kind of owner suits a Clumber best? Whilst all dogs need attention and thrive on their owners' devotion, a Clumber truly blossoms when he is well loved. The more time you give to him, the more devoted he will become. The word 'loyal' appears in the standard, but Clumbers are loyal whilst their owner is present and will transfer their love to almost anyone who will give them the time and the care to which they are accustomed. This should not diminish the love that owners feel, because looking into the face of a Clumber is a pleasure few things can match.

Clumbers blossom when given a home filled with love.

The ideal situation for the happiest Clumber and the happiest owner is a house with easy access to a securely fenced garden, with adequate shade and room to frolic. A Clumber can live in the city in a flat, but will require several good walks a day.

Children must be instructed to respect the Clumber Spaniel from puppyhood. This young lady has a lovely rapport with these puppies.

It cannot be stressed enough that buying a dog is a commitment; leaving a dog alone for very long periods of time on a regular basis, tying it outside or keeping it in the garage or basement are not options in a satisfactory dog household. With any dog, and especially a Clumber, the prospective dog owner must be honest about his reasons for wanting a dog. An ethical breeder will take a dog back, but the animal shelters are full of dogs that were purchased for the wrong reasons and discarded. It is better to think about the possible problems of dog ownership before you get the dog.

The Clumber is a versatile dog excelling in the field, working well in obedience, showing off in the show ring, learning agility, tracking and just loving his family. If you want to be entertained all the time, and constantly be the focus of adoring, mischievous eyes, this is the breed for you.

HEALTH CONSIDERATIONS

Clumbers on the whole are healthy, but some consideration must be given to problems that do exist in the breed. Back and neck problems are the conditions that most concern breeders and fanciers. You, as an owner, can use common sense in helping to eliminate situations that may possibly bring on an incidence of a disk problem. It is best not to expect a Clumber to jump down from any high place. A child must never ride on a Clumber's back or attempt anything similar that can endanger those parts of the dog's body. Clumbers can have eye problems, such as dry eye, that can require prolonged treatment with eye drops. Clumbers in the past have been very prone to hip dysplasia, but with the co-operation of breeders, the incidence of this condition has been decreased. It must be remembered that since this is a rare breed, the gene pool is small and it has been difficult to eradicate the breed of some hereditary conditions.

Be certain the parents of your Clumber puppies have healthy, clear eyes.

The small size of the gene pool underlines the importance of finding a reputable breeder, one who pays attention to proper breeding practices, studies the breed and keeps up on the latest medical technology. The buyer of a pet may feel that all of this is not important to him or his dog, but only a healthy dog can be a truly happy one, and the owner will also be happier (and wealthier) if his dog has no health problems and lives a long time.

The life expectancy of a Clumber has lengthened in the last 20 years. If the unpredictable does not happen, you can expect your Clumber to live to be 11 or 12 and sometimes beyond that to 13 or more years, if you are very lucky. The more attention you pay to your dog, and the more you observe him and learn about him, the healthier he will be and the longer he will live.

It has been stressed, and

Few dogs are as comical as the Clumber. This gentleman is an expert duck hunter!

cannot be stressed enough, that there is a partnership between the dog and the owner. The Clumber brings to this relationship inherent canine qualities with the special characteristics of its particular breed. A dog, however, is somewhat helpless in the human world and cannot provide its own food, shelter or medical care; it must depend on its owner for these tangible things. It must also depend on its owner for the intangible—love. The dog's owner, once he has decided to share his world, must be willing to live up to this commitment. An investment in a Clumber Spaniel will bring forth much more profit in the form of unconditional, non-judgmental love than you could have hoped for.

BREED STANDARD FOR THE CLUMBER SPANIEL

A breed standard is the official description of the way a dog should look and act. Once written and agreed upon, it becomes the accepted 'bible' for breeders and judges to evaluate the quality of specimens of the breed to which it refers. Dogs shown in exhibition are compared to the breed standard. Only those dogs that 'stack up' to the standard will earn the title of champion and are therefore worthy of breeding.

Whilst the standard is subject to the interpretation of the judge and breeder, it does attempt to emphasise the most important aspects of the dog.

The standard varies from place to place. Throughout the United Kingdom, The Kennel Club's standard is the accepted standard. Throughout the European Union nations, the standard of the Fédération Cynologique Internationale is the accepted standard.

The head of the Clumber Spaniel is its unique feature; it must be square, massive and broad on top.

THE KENNEL CLUB STANDARD FOR THE CLUMBER SPANIEL

General Appearance: Well balanced, heavily boned, active with a thoughtful expression, overall appearance denoting strength.

Characteristics: Stoical, great-hearted, highly intelligent with a determined attitude enhancing his natural ability. A silent worker with an excellent nose.

Temperament: Steady, reliable, kind and dignified; more aloof than other Spaniels, showing no tendency towards aggression.

Head and Skull: Square, massive, medium length, broad on top with decided occiput; heavy brows; deep stop. Heavy, square muzzle with well developed flews. No exaggeration in head and skull.

The neck should be long and thick. It must express power. The forequarters display strong shoulders with short, straight legs.

The ideal Clumber back is straight, broad and long.

Eyes: Clean, dark amber, slightly sunk, some haw showing but without excess. Full light eyes highly undesirable.

Ears: Large, vine leaf-shaped, well covered with straight hair. Hanging slightly forward, feather not to extend below leather.

Mouth: Jaws strong, with a perfect, regular and complete scissor bite, i.e. upper teeth closely overlapping lower teeth and set square to the jaws.

Neck: Fairly long, thick, powerful.

Forequarters: Shoulders strong, sloping, muscular; legs short, straight, well boned, strong.

Body: Long, heavy, near to ground. Chest deep. Well sprung ribs. Back straight, broad, long. Muscular loin, well let down in flank.

Hindquarters: Very powerful and well developed. Hocks low, stifles well bent and set straight.

Dogs competing in the show ring are compared to the breed standard. It is the judge's responsibility to know the standard to determine how closely each dog conforms to the standard.

A young show-quality Clumber Spaniel being taught the typical show pose.

Feet: Large, round, well covered with hair.

Tail: Set low, well feathered, carried level with back.

Gait/Movement: Rolling gait attributable to long body and short legs. Moving straight fore and aft, with effortless drive.

Coat: Abundant, close, silky and straight. Legs and chest well feathered.

Colour: Plain white body preferred, with lemon markings; orange permissible. Slight head markings and freckled muzzle.

A good eye lid formation exhibited by an adult Clumber.

Am Ch Raycroft Springsteen TD is a handsome and accomplished Clumber who lives in the Great Lake region of the USA. The suffix TD is an American Kennel Club title for Tracking Dog.

Size: Ideal weight: dogs: 36 kgs (80 lbs); bitches: 29.5 kgs (65 lbs).

Faults: Any departure from the foregoing points should be considered a fault and the seriousness with which the fault should be regarded should be in exact proportion to its degree.

Note: Male animals should have two apparently normal testicles fully descended into the scrotum.

A Clumber Spaniel winning an 'Award of Merit' at an American National Specialty. Owner, Janice Friis.

YOUR PUPPY
CLUMBER SPANIEL

OWNER CONSIDERATIONS

Although the reader of these pages is more likely interested in finding a companionable and family animal than a show prospect, there remain many serious factors governing your choice of a Clumber Spaniel puppy. A primary consideration is time, not only the time of the animal's allotted lifespan, which is often well over twelve years, but also the time required for the owner to exercise and care for the creature. If you are not committed to the welfare and whole existence of this energetic, purposeful animal; if, in the simplest, most basic example, you are not willing to walk your dog daily, no matter what the weather, do not choose a Clumber Spaniel as a companion. Perhaps in that case you are actually not ready for a dog at all, because they are living beings whose every need depends on you!

Space is another important consideration. The Clumber Spaniel in early puppyhood may be well accommodated in a corner of your kitchen, but an adult Clumber may weigh 36 kgs and larger space may well be required. A garden with a fence is also a basic and reasonable expectation. Many breeders will not sell a dog to a home that does not have a fenced property.

Along with these factors there are the usual problems associated with puppies of any breed, like the damages likely to be sustained by your floors, furniture and, not least of all, to your freedom (of movement), as in holiday or weekend trips. This union is a serious affair and should be considered with family input.

This Clumber puppy is only four weeks of age. Note how beautifully shaped this youngster's head is.

DID YOU KNOW?

Unfortunately, when a puppy is bought by someone who does not take into consideration the time and attention that dog ownership requires, it is the puppy who suffers when he is either abandoned or placed in a shelter by a frustrated owner. So all of the 'homework' you do in preparation for your pup's arrival will benefit you both. The more informed you are, the more

you will know what to expect and the better equipped you will be to handle the ups and downs of raising a puppy. Hopefully, everyone in the household is willing to do his part in raising and caring for the pup. The anticipation of owning a dog often brings a lot of promises from excited family members: 'I will walk him every day,' 'I will feed him,' 'I will housebreak him,' etc., but these things take time and effort, and promises can easily be forgotten once the novelty of the new pet has worn off.

Once you decide to add a dog to your family, a Clumber Spaniel can be perhaps the most rewarding of all breeds. (The fancier of each breed will tell you the same thing.) A few suggestions will help in buying your dog.

ACQUIRING A PUPPY

The safest method of obtaining your puppy is to seek out a reputable breeder. This is suggested even if you are not looking for a show specimen. The Kennel Club is able to recommend breeders of quality Clumber Spaniels, as can any local all-breed club or Clumber Spaniel club. You should be able to find the name of the secretary of that club from The Kennel Club or the national dog organisation of your country. In this modern age, most canine organisations can be found online on your computer. The novice breeders and pet owners who advertise at attractive prices in the local newspapers are probably kind enough toward their dogs, but perhaps do not have the expertise or the facilities required to successfully raise these animals.

There are many reasons that you should choose to buy a puppy from a breeder. One of the most important is that a reputable breeder will stand behind his dogs. A breeder may also be an important source of advice and

DID YOU KNOW?

Your puppy should have a well-fed appearance but not a distended abdomen, which may indicate worms

or incorrect feeding, or both. The body should be firm, with a solid feel. The skin of the abdomen should be pale pink and clean, without signs of scratching or rash. Check the hind legs to make certain that dewclaws were removed, if any were present at birth.

assistance if you have a problem or a question as you raise your Clumber Spaniel. The most reputable breeders are interested to see how their extended family turns out.

It is seldom that a breeder would sell a puppy before it is at least ten weeks old. A novice dog owner would certainly not be capable of taking care of a younger puppy. The vaccination schedule is very specific and the first shots are certainly the responsibility of the breeder.

A big question for many prospective puppy buyers is the sex of the dog. Many people favour males because they feel them to be more affectionate. If you decide on a female, she should certainly be spayed if she is going to be a pet. This will be better for her future health and much easier for the family. Either sex can and will be an excellent pet if you do your part.

If you are convinced that the

DID YOU KNOW?

Your selection of a good puppy can be determined by your needs. A show potential or a good pet? It is your choice. Every puppy, however,

should be of good temperament. Although show-quality puppies are bred and raised with emphasis on physical conformation, responsible breeders strive for equally good temperament. Do not buy from a breeder who concentrates solely on physical beauty at the expense of personality.

Clumber Spaniel is the ideal dog for you, it's time to learn about where to find a puppy and what to look for. Since Clumber Spaniels are relatively rare, usually the breeder chooses the puppy he feels is appropriate for your family, or for the function the dog will serve. Many times the breeder will send photos and a video to show you what is available. Buying a dog of a rare breed is a very different prospect than buying a popular one, which can often be found quite nearby. There are even times when the prospective puppy buyer may be put on a waiting list. It is often the measure of just how much you want this particular breed

Locating a litter of Clumber Spaniels may take some time for the new owner. You should enquire about breeders who enjoy a good reputation in the breed. You are looking for an established breeder with outstanding dog ethics and a strong commitment to the breed. New owners should have as

DID YOU KNOW?

Breeders rarely release puppies until they are eight to ten weeks of age. This is an acceptable age for most breeds of dog, excepting toy breeds, which are not released until around 12 weeks, given their petite sizes. If a breeder has a puppy that is 12 weeks or more, it is likely well socialised and housetrained. Be sure that it is otherwise healthy before deciding to take it home.

INSURANCE

Many good breeders will offer you insurance with your new puppy, which is an excellent idea. The first few weeks of insurance will probably be covered free of charge or with only minimal cost, allowing you to take up the policy when this expires. If you own a pet dog, it is sensible to take out such a policy as veterinary fees can be high, although routine vaccinations and boosters are not covered. Look carefully at the many options open to you before deciding which suits you best.

many questions as they have doubts. An established breeder is indeed the one to answer your four million questions and make you comfortable with your choice of the Clumber Spaniel. An established breeder will sell you a puppy at a fair price if, and only if, the breeder determines that you are a suitable, worthy owner of his/her dogs. An established breeder can be relied upon for advice, no matter what time of day or night. A reputable breeder will accept a puppy back, without questions, should you decide that this not the right dog for you.

Choosing a breeder is an important first step in dog ownership. Fortunately, the majority of Clumber Spaniel breeders are devoted to the breed and its well being. Potential owners are encouraged to attend dog shows to see the Clumber Spaniels in action, to meet the handlers firsthand and to get an idea of what Clumbers look like outside a photographer's lens. Provided you approach the handlers when they are not terribly busy with the dogs, most are more than willing to answer questions, recommend breeders and give advice.

Locating a dam with a nice litter of Clumber Spaniel puppies will require that you do your homework. Contact The Kennel Club for breeder referrals.

Visit the litter to evaluate the condition of the puppies and dam as far as cleanliness, friendliness and conformation to the standard. Whether or not you intend to show your Clumber, you want it to grow up looking and acting like a Clumber.

When choosing a breeder, reputation is much more important than convenience of location. You may be well advised to avoid the novice who lives only a couple miles away. The local novice breeder, trying so hard to get rid of that first litter of puppies, is more than accommodating and anxious to sell you one. That breeder will charge you as much as any established breeder. The novice breeder isn't going to interrogate you and your family about your intentions with the puppy, the environment and training you can provide, etc. That breeder will be nowhere to be found when your poorly bred, badly adjusted four-pawed monster starts to growl and spit up at midnight or eat the family cat!

Keeping in mind that many top breeders have waiting lists, sometimes new owners have to wait as long as two years for a puppy. If you are really committed to the breeder whom you've selected, then you will wait (and hope for an early arrival!). If not, you may have to resort to your second- or third-choice breeder. Don't be too

DID YOU KNOW?

You should not even think about buying a puppy that looks sick, undernourished, overly frightened or nervous. Sometimes a timid puppy will warm up to you after a 30-minute 'let's-get-acquainted' session.

anxious, however. If the breeder doesn't have any waiting list, or any customers, there is probably a good reason.

Now that you have contacted and met a breeder or two and made your choice about which breeder is best suited to your needs, it's time to visit the litter. If you do go to a breeder's home to choose your puppy, consider the environment in which the puppies are raised. The puppies should be clean and the pen and area in which they are kept should be as free of faeces and other debris as possible. You should take note if there are toys for the puppies and whether they had a clean bowl of water. If there are scabs or caked dirt or faeces on the puppy, or if it is matted or has crusty debris in its eyes, common sense should tell you that this puppy has not had the care required to raise a healthy

DOCUMENTATION

Two important documents you will get from the breeder are the pup's pedigree and registration certificate. The breeder should register the litter and each pup with The Kennel Club, and it is

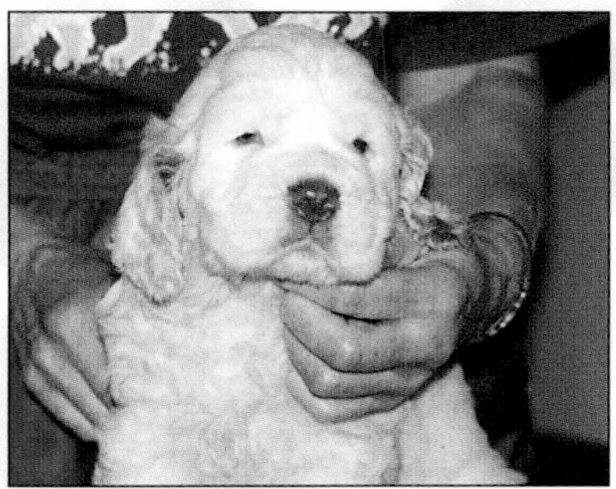

necessary for you to have the paperwork if you plan on showing or breeding in the future.

Make sure you know the breeder's intentions on which type of registration he will obtain for the pup. There are limited registrations which may prohibit the dog from being shown, bred or from competing in non-conformation trials such as Working or Agility if the breeder feels that the pup is not of sufficient quality to do so. There is also a type of registration that will permit the dog in non-conformation competition only.

On the reverse side of the registration certificate, the new owner can find the transfer section which must be signed by the breeder.

Finding a quality, healthy Clumber puppy will be worth all the effort that you invest.

The puppy will probably look and act like its dam. This pup is taking his mum for a walk!

and well-adjusted animal. Do not succumb to this puppy because you are sorry for it. You will be sorry you did in the end.

If you do get a chance to visit the litter and choose your own puppy, it is helpful to see the mother and her interaction with her puppies and with her owner. In fact if you do get to see a litter, do not purchase a puppy without first seeing the mother. Sometimes you may get to see the father also, but often the breeder has used a stud dog belonging to another breeder. You will want to look for an alert puppy, one which is moving around and playing with the others. The puppy should have no tendency to stumble or drag its feet. Look at the mouth to make sure the bite is fairly even, although maturity can correct errors present in puppyhood. If you have any doubt, ask to see the mother's mouth. However, if you are looking for a pet puppy, a mouth that is not totally correct will not be a hindrance in the dog's life. In fact, sometimes a breeder will sell a dog as a pet rather than a show prospect just because its bite (position of the teeth) is not perfect. With a Clumber you may find that a breeder may offer you a puppy with more colour than it desirable, which of course would not affect your family's enjoyment at all.

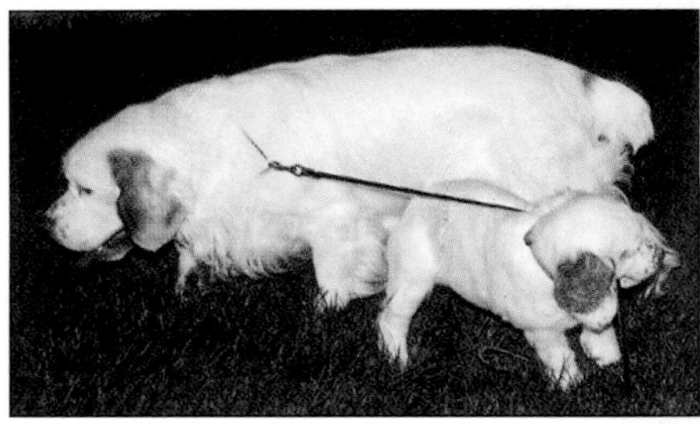

Clumber Spaniels generally have large litters, averaging seven puppies, so selection is good once you have located a desirable litter. Neither the basic structure of the

DID YOU KNOW?

If you lead an erratic, unpredictable life, with daily or weekly changes in your work requirements, consider the problems of owning a puppy. The new puppy has to be fed regularly, socialised (loved, petted, handled, introduced to other people) and, most importantly, allowed to visit outdoors for toilet training. As the dog gets older, it can be more tolerant of deviations in its feeding and toilet relief.

breed nor the temperament has much variation, nonetheless, beware of the shy or overly aggressive puppy and be especially conscious of the nervous Clumber Spaniel pup. Don't let sentiment or emotion trap you into buying the runt of the litter.

Breeders commonly allow visitors to see the litter by around the fifth or sixth week, and puppies leave for their new homes between the eighth and tenth week. Breeders who permit their puppies to leave early are more interested in your pounds than their puppies' well being. Puppies need to learn the rules of the trade from their dams, and most dams continue teaching the pups manners, and do's and don'ts, until around the eighth week. Breeders spend significant amounts of time with the Clumber Spaniel toddlers so that they are able to interact with the 'other species', i.e. humans. Given the long history that dogs and humans have, bonding between the two species is natural but must be nurtured. A well-bred, well-socialised Clumber Spaniel pup wants nothing more than to be near you and please you.

A rare peek at a three-day-old Clumber litter. Obliging our visit is Am Ch Critter's Leap of Faith, CGC. Breeders usually don't allow visitors to see the litter until the puppies are five or six weeks old.

ARE YOU A FIT OWNER?

If the breeder from whom you are buying a puppy asks you a lot of personal questions, do not be insulted. Such a breeder wants to be sure that you will be a fit provider for his puppy.

COMMITMENT OF OWNERSHIP

After considering all of these factors, you have most likely already made some very important decisions about selecting your puppy. You have chosen a Clumber Spaniel, which means that you have decided which characteristics you want in a dog and what type of dog will best fit into your family and lifestyle. If you have selected a breeder, you have gone a step further—you have done your research and found a responsible, conscientious person who breeds quality Clumber Spaniel and who should be a reliable source of help as you and your puppy adjust to life together. If you have observed a litter in action, you have obtained a firsthand look at the dynamics of a puppy 'pack' and, thus, you should learn about each pup's individual personality—perhaps you have even found one that particularly appeals to you.

However, even if you have not yet found the Clumber Spaniel puppy of your dreams, observing pups will help you learn to recognise certain behaviour and to determine what a pup's behaviour indicates about his temperament. You will be able to pick out which pups are the leaders, which ones are less outgoing, which ones are confident, which ones are shy, playful, friendly, aggressive, etc. Equally as important, you will learn to recognise what a healthy pup should look and act like. All of these things will help you in your search, and when you find the Clumber Spaniel that was meant for you, you will know it!

Researching your breed, selecting a responsible breeder and observing as many pups as possible are all important steps on the way to Clumber ownership. It may seem like a lot of effort...and you have not even brought the pup home yet! Remember, though, you cannot be too careful when it comes to deciding on the type of dog you want and finding out about your prospective pup's background. Buying a puppy is not—or should not be—just another whimsical purchase. This is one instance in which you actually do get to choose your own family! You may be thinking that buying a puppy should be fun—it should not be so serious and so much work. Keep in mind that your puppy is not a cuddly stuffed toy or decorative lawn ornament, but a creature that will become a real member of your family. You will come to realise that, whilst buying a puppy is a pleasurable and exciting endeavour, it is not something to be taken lightly. Relax...the fun will start when the pup comes home!

Always keep in mind that a puppy is nothing more than a baby in a furry disguise...a baby who is virtually helpless in a human world and who trusts his owner for fulfilment of his basic

needs for survival. In addition to water and shelter, your pup needs care, protection, guidance and love. If you are not prepared to commit to this, then you are not prepared to own a dog.

PREPARING PUPPY'S PLACE IN YOUR HOME

Researching your breed and finding a breeder are only two aspects of the 'homework' you will have to do before bringing your Clumber Spaniel puppy home. You will also have to prepare your home and family for the new addition. Much as you would prepare a nursery for a newborn baby, you will need to designate a place in your home that will be the puppy's own. How you prepare your home will depend on how much freedom the pup will be allowed. Whatever you decide, you must ensure that he has a place that he can 'call his own.' The ideal situation for a Clumber is to spend a good part of the day outside, and the rest in the house with the family.

When you bring your new puppy into your home, you are bringing him into what will become his home as well. Obviously, you did not buy a puppy so that he could take over your house, but in order for a puppy to grow into a stable, well-adjusted dog, he has to feel comfortable in his surroundings. Remember, he is leaving the warmth and security of his mother and littermates, as well as the familiarity of the only place he has ever known, so it is important to make his transition as easy as possible. By preparing a place in your home for the puppy, you are making him feel as welcome as possible in a strange new place. It should not take him long to get used to it, but the sudden shock of being transplanted is somewhat traumatic for a young pup. Imagine how a small child would feel in the same situation—that is how your puppy must be feeling. It is up to you to reassure him and to let him know, 'Little chap, you are going to like it here!'

These Clumber puppies are ready for their new homes. Making a choice is never easy with puppies of the same quality, temperament and size. Make up your mind as to the sex of the dog that you want.

PHOTO COURTESY OF DOSKOCIL.

Your local pet shop should have the crate that will best suit your Clumber puppy.

WHAT YOU SHOULD BUY

CRATE

To someone unfamiliar with the use of crates in dog training, it may seem like punishment to shut a dog in a crate, but this is not the case at all. Although all breeders do not advocate crate training, more and more breeders and

CRATE TRAINING TIPS

During crate training, you should partition off the section of the crate in which the pup stays. If he is given too big an area, this will hinder your training efforts. Crate training is

based on the fact that a dog does not like to soil his sleeping quarters, so it is ineffective to keep a pup in a crate that is so big that he can eliminate in one end and get far enough away from it to sleep. Also, you want to make the crate den-like for the pup. Blankets and a favourite toy will make the crate cosy for the small pup; as he grows, you may want to evict some of his 'roommates' to make more room.

It will take some coaxing at first, but be patient. Given some time to get used to it, your pup will adapt to his new home-within-a-home quite nicely.

trainers are recommending crates as a preferred tool for pet puppies as well as show puppies. Crates are not cruel—crates have many humane and highly effective uses in dog care and training. For example, crate training is a very popular and very successful housebreaking method. A crate keeps your dog safe during travel, and, perhaps most importantly, a crate provides your dog with a place of his own in your home. It serves as a 'doggie bedroom' of sorts—your Clumber Spaniel can curl up in his crate when he wants to sleep or when he just needs a break. Many dogs sleep in their crates overnight. When lined with soft bedding and his favourite toy, a crate becomes a cosy pseudo-den for your dog. Like his ancestors, he too will seek out the comfort and retreat of a den—you just happen to be providing him with something a little more luxurious than his early ancestors enjoyed.

As far as purchasing a crate, the type that you buy is up to you. It will most likely be one of the two most popular types: wire or

Once the Clumber Spaniel becomes accustomed to his crate, he will use it for nap time. The crate may have a removable door.

Crates are available in many sizes, styles and materials from which they are constructed.

fibreglass. There are advantages and disadvantages to each type. For example, a wire crate is more open, allowing the air to flow through and affording the dog a view of what is going on around him. A fibreglass crate, however, is sturdier for airline travel since it provides more protection for the dog; it is not good for a permanent crate because it retains the heat and the dog is too closed in. The size of the crate is another thing to consider. Puppies do not stay puppies forever—in fact, sometimes it seems as if they grow right before your eyes. A small crate may be fine for a very young Clumber Spaniel pup, but it will not do him much good for long! Unless you have the money and the inclination to buy a new crate every time your pup has a growth spurt, it is better to get one that will accommodate your dog both as a pup and at full size. It is a cruel torture for a dog to be in a crate that is too small for it. Remember a Clumber can weigh as much as 36 kgs.

Once housetrained, your Clumber will be able to enjoy greater freedom about the house. This Clumber enjoys napping on a doggie pillow.

Bedding

Veterinary bedding in the dog's crate will help the dog feel more at home and you may also like to pop in a small blanket, although he will probably chew it. This will take the place of the leaves, twigs, etc., that the pup would use in the wild to make a den; the pup can make his own 'burrow' in the crate. Although your pup is far removed from his den-making ancestors, the denning instinct is still a part of his genetic makeup. Second, until you take your pup home, he has been sleeping amidst the warmth of his mother and littermates, and whilst a blanket is not the same as a warm, breathing body, it still provides heat and something with which to snuggle. You will want to wash your pup's bedding frequently in case he has an accident in his crate, and replace or remove any blanket that becomes ragged and starts to fall apart.

Toys

Toys are a must for dogs of all ages, especially for curious playful pups. Puppies are the 'children' of the dog world, and what child does not love toys? Chew toys provide enjoyment to both dog and owner—your dog will enjoy playing with his favourite toys, whilst you will enjoy the fact that they distract him from your expensive shoes and leather sofa. Puppies love to chew; in fact, chewing is a physical need for pups as they are teething, and everything looks appetising! The full range of your possessions—from old tea towel to Oriental carpet—is fair game in the eyes of a teething pup. Puppies are not all that discerning when it comes to finding something to literally 'sink their teeth into'—everything tastes great! A great toy for an active dog is a football. It is also a good exerciser as the dog will probably kick it and chase after it. You must remember to check your dog's toys often to determine if

TOYS, TOYS, TOYS!

With a big variety of dog toys available, and so many that look like they would be a lot of fun for a dog, be careful in your selection. It is amazing what a set of puppy teeth can do to an innocent-looking toy, so, obviously, safety is a major consideration. Be sure to choose the most durable products that you can find. Hard nylon bones and toys are a safe bet, and many of them are offered in different scents and flavours that will be sure to capture your dog's attention. It is always fun to play a game of catch with your dog, and there are balls and flying discs that are specially made to withstand dog teeth.

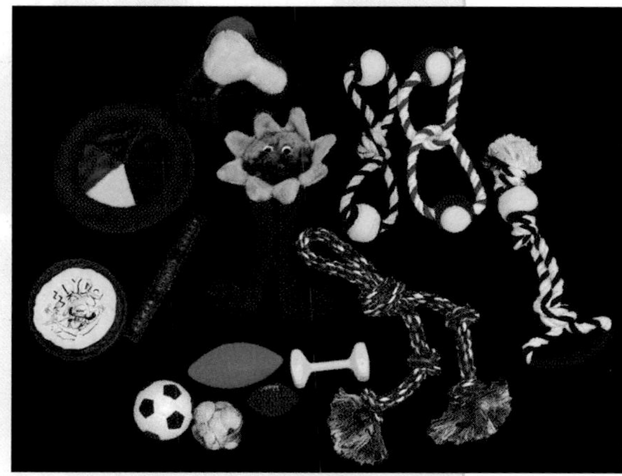

Never offer children's toys to your Clumber. These toys are not designed to withstand the power of a dog's teeth and can be destroyed easily.

they have started to chew them up. If so, throw them away.

Stuffed toys are another option: these are good to put in the dog's crate to give him some company. Be careful of these, as a pup can destuff one pretty quickly. For your own sake, stay away from those stuffed with sand or chopped foam, both of which will get all over your home. Avoid stuffed toys with small plastic eyes or other small parts that a pup can choke on.

Similarly, squeaky toys are quite popular, but must be avoided for the Clumber Spaniel. Perhaps a squeaky toy can be used as an aid in training, but not for free play. If a pup 'disembowels' one of these, the small plastic squeaker inside can be dangerous if swallowed. Latex squeaky toys do last longer than hard plastic ones, which a Clumber can chew apart in minutes. Never give rawhide to your dog because enough chewing can soften it and the piece can be partially swallowed and stick in the dog's throat.

Raw natural marrow bones with most of the marrow removed (it's too rich for a pup) make the best and cheapest toy. Ask the butcher for the ones with the thickest edge and don't have any splintery pieces on the sides. When the last bit of marrow is

DID YOU KNOW?

Some experts in canine health advise that stress during a dog's early years of development can compromise and weaken his immune system and

may trigger the potential for a shortened life expectancy. They emphasise the need for happy and stress-free growing-up years.

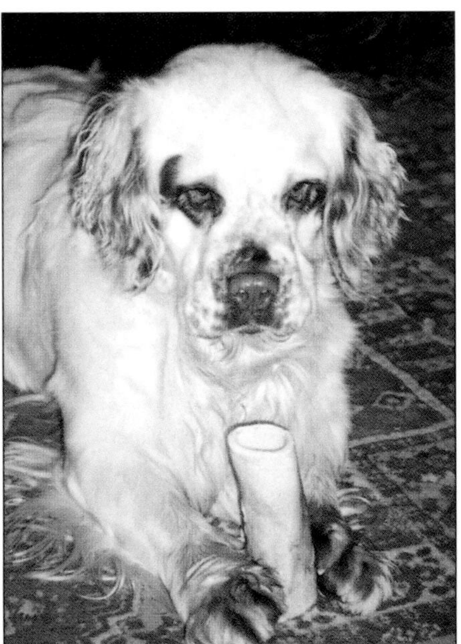

Raw marrow bones are very satisfactory as dog chews. Monitor your dog closely whenever he has a chew bone.

Your local pet shop will usually have a wide selection of collars and leads from which you can make a choice.

gone and the dog has lost interest in it, you can put a piece of cheese or some peanut butter in the middle of the bone, and the dog will chew on it sometimes for hours.

Monitor the condition of all your pup's toys carefully and get rid of any that have been chewed to the point of becoming potentially dangerous.

Lead

A nylon lead is probably the best option as it is the most resistant to puppy teeth should your pup take a liking to chewing on his lead. Of course, this is a habit that should be 'nipped' in the bud, but if your pup likes to chew on his lead he has a very slim chance of being able to chew through the strong nylon. Nylon leads are also lightweight, which is good for a young Clumber Spaniel who is just getting used to the idea of walking on a lead. For everyday walking and safety purposes, the nylon lead is a good choice. As your pup grows up and gets used to walking on the lead, you may want to purchase a flexible lead. These leads allow you to extend the length to give the dog a broader area to explore or to shorten the length to keep the dog

FINANCIAL RESPONSIBILITY

Grooming tools, collars, leashes, dog beds and, of course, toys will be an expense to you when you first obtain your pup, and the cost will

continue throughout your dog's lifetime. If your puppy damages or destroys your possessions (as most puppies surely will!) or something belonging to a neighbour, you can calculate additional expense. There is also flea and pest control, which every dog owner faces more than once. You must be able to handle the financial responsibility of owning a dog.

The BUCKLE COLLAR is the standard collar used for everyday purpose. Be sure that you adjust the buckle on growing puppies. Check it every day. It can become too tight overnight! These collars can be made of leather or nylon. Attach your dog's identification tags to this collar.

The CHOKE COLLAR is the usual collar recommended for training. It is constructed of highly polished steel so that it slides easily through the stainless steel loop. The idea is that the dog controls the pressure around its neck and he will stop pulling if the collar becomes uncomfortable. Never leave a choke collar on your dog when not training.

The HALTER is for a trained dog that has to be restrained to prevent running away, chasing a cat and the like. Considered the most humane of all collars, it is frequently used on smaller dogs for which collars are not comfortable.

close to you. Of course, there are also special leads for training purposes.

Collar

Your pup should get used to wearing a collar all the time since you will want to attach his ID tags to it. You have to attach the lead to something! A lightweight nylon collar is a good choice; make sure that it fits snugly enough so that the pup cannot wriggle out of it, but is loose enough so that it will not be uncomfortably tight around the pup's neck. You should be able to fit a finger between the pup and the collar. It may take some time for your pup to get used to wearing the collar, but soon he will not even notice that it is there. Choke collars are made for training, but should only be used by an experienced handler.

DID YOU KNOW?

It will take at least two weeks for your puppy to become accustomed to his new surroundings. Give him

lots of love, attention, handling, frequent opportunities to relieve himself, a diet he likes to eat and a place he can call his own.

Choose your Clumber's water and food bowls wisely. These everyday items should endure many years of use.

Food and Water Bowls

Your pup will need two bowls, one for food and one for water. You may want two sets of bowls, one for inside and one for outside. Stainless steel bowls are the safest and best. Plastic bowls are more chewable. Dogs tend not to chew on the steel variety, which can be sterilised. It is important to buy

Your local pet shop sells an array of dishes and bowls for water and food.

Photo courtesy of Mikki Pet products

sturdy bowls since anything is in danger of being chewed by puppy teeth and you do not want your dog to be constantly chewing apart his bowl (for his safety and for your purse!).

Cleaning Supplies

Until a pup is housetrained, you will be doing a lot of cleaning. Accidents will occur, which is okay in the beginning because the puppy does not know any better. All you can do is be prepared to clean up any 'accidents.' Old rags, towels, newspapers and a safe disinfectant are good to have on hand.

Beyond the Basics

The items previously discussed are the bare necessities. You will find out what else you need as you go along—grooming supplies, flea/tick protection, baby gates to partition a room, etc. These things will vary depending on your situation but it is important that

PUPPY-PROOFING

Thoroughly puppy-proof your house before bringing your puppy home. Never use roach or rodent poisons in any area accessible to the puppy. Avoid the use of toilet cleaners. Most dogs are born with 'toilet sonar' and will take a drink if the lid is left open. Also keep the rubbish secured and out of reach.

CHEMICAL TOXINS

Scour your garage for potential puppy dangers. Remove weed killers, pesticides and antifreeze materials. Antifreeze is highly toxic and even a few drops can kill an adult dog. The sweet taste attracts the animal, who will quickly consume it from the floor or curbside.

you have everything you need to feed and make your Clumber Spaniel comfortable in his first few days at home.

PUPPY-PROOFING YOUR HOME

Aside from making sure that your Clumber Spaniel will be comfortable in your home, you also have to make sure that your home is safe for your Clumber Spaniel. This means taking precautions that your pup will not get into anything he should not get into and that there is nothing within his reach that may harm him should he sniff it, chew it, inspect it, etc. This probably seems obvious since, whilst you are primarily concerned with your pup's safety, at the same time you do not want your belongings to be ruined. Breakables should be placed out of reach if your dog is to have full run of the house. If he is to be limited to certain places within the house, keep any potentially dangerous items in the 'off-limits' areas. An electrical cord can pose a danger should the puppy decide to taste it—and who is going to convince a pup that it would not make a great chew toy? Cords should be fastened tightly against the wall. If your dog is going to spend time in a crate, make sure that there is nothing near his crate that he can reach if he sticks his curious little nose or paws through the openings. Just as you would with a child, keep all household cleaners and chemicals where the pup cannot get to them.

It is also important to make sure that the outside of your home is safe. The best way for a puppy to enjoy the outdoors and be safe is to have a fenced pen with gravel or crushed stone on the

It is your responsibility to clean up after your dog has relieved himself. Pet shops have various aids to assist in the cleanup job.

Fences give owners a false sense of security. Always be aware of the condition of the fence that surrounds your property.

bottom. There must be access to shade, but a puppy can be left there unattended (with toys) for short periods of time which can be increased as it gets older. No Clumber should ever be left tied to anything. Do not let a fence give you a false sense of security; you would be surprised how crafty (and persistent) a dog can be in working out how to dig under and squeeze his way through small holes, or to jump or climb over a fence. The remedy is to make the fence high enough so that it really is impossible for

your dog to get over it (about 2 metres should suffice), and well embedded into the ground. Be sure to repair or secure any gaps in the fence. Check the fence periodically to ensure that it is in good shape and make repairs as needed; a very determined pup may return to the same spot to 'work on it' until he is able to get through.

DID YOU KNOW?

You will probably start feeding your pup the same food that he has been getting from the breeder; the breeder

should give you a few days' supply to start you off. Although you should not give your pup too many treats, you will want to have puppy treats on hand for coaxing, training, rewards, etc. Be careful, though, as a small pup's calorie requirements are relatively low and a few treats can add up to almost a full day's worth of calories without the required nutrition.

FIRST TRIP TO THE VET

You have picked out your puppy, and your home and family are ready. Now all you have to do is collect your Clumber Spaniel from the breeder and the fun begins, right? Well...not so fast. Something else you need to prepare is your pup's first trip to the veterinary surgeon. Perhaps the breeder can recommend someone in the area who specialises in Clumber Spaniels. If that is not possible, ask someone you trust who has a healthy dog. Either way, you should have an appointment arranged for your pup before you pick him up and plan on taking him for an examination before taking him home.

The pup's first visit will consist of an overall examination to make sure that the pup does not have any problems that are not apparent to the vet's eye. The veterinary surgeon will also set up a schedule for the pup's vaccinations; the breeder will inform you of which ones the pup has already received and the vet can continue from there.

DID YOU KNOW?

Taking your dog from the breeder to your home in a car can be a very uncomfortable experience for both

of you. The puppy will have been taken from his warm, friendly, safe environment and brought into a strange new environment. An environment that moves! Be prepared for loose bowels, urination, crying, whining and even fear biting. With proper love and encouragement when you arrive home, the stress of the trip should quickly disappear.

INTRODUCTION TO THE FAMILY

Everyone in the house will be excited about the puppy coming home and will want to pet him and play with him, but it is best to make the introduction low-key so as not to overwhelm the puppy. He is apprehensive already. It is the first time he has been separated from his mother and the breeder, and the ride to your home is likely the first time he has been in a car. The last thing you want to do is smother him, as this will only frighten him further. This is not to say that human contact is not extremely necessary at this stage, because this is the time when a connection between the pup and his human family is formed. Gentle petting and soothing words should help console him, as well as just putting him down and letting him explore on his own (under your watchful eye, of course).

The pup may approach the family members or may busy himself with exploring for a while. Gradually, each person should spend some time with the pup, one at a time, crouching down to get as close to the pup's level as possible whilst petting him gently and letting him sniff each person's hands. Remember

This is what life with a Clumber is all about. It is a loved, trusted member of the family. It plays this role magnificently well.

that the pup is experiencing a lot of things for the first time, at the same time. There are new people, new noises, new smells, and new things to investigate: so be gentle, be affectionate, and be as comforting as you can be.

YOUR PUP'S FIRST NIGHT HOME

You have travelled home with your new charge safely in his crate or a family member's lap. He's been to the vet for a thorough check-up; he's been weighed, his papers examined; perhaps he's even been vaccinated and wormed as well. He's met the family, including the excited children and the less-than-happy cat. He's explored his area, his new bed, the garden and anywhere else he's been permitted. He's eaten his first meal at home and relieved himself in the proper place. He's heard lots of new sounds, smelled new friends and seen more of the outside world than ever before.

That was just the first day! He's worn out and is ready for bed...or so you think!

It's puppy's first night and you are ready to say 'Good night'—keep in mind that this is puppy's first night ever to be sleeping alone. His dam and littermates are no longer at paw's length and he's a bit scared, cold and lonely. Be reassuring to your new family member. This is not the time to spoil him and give in to his inevitable whining.

Puppies whine. They whine to let the others know where they are and hopefully to get company out of it. Place your pup in his new bed or crate in his room and close the door. Mercifully, he may fall asleep without a peep. When the inevitable occurs, ignore the whining: he is fine. Be strong and keep his interest in mind. Do not allow your heart to become guilty and visit the pup. He will fall asleep.

Who could resist the pleas of a Clumber puppy? Always keep in mind that you are the 'top dog' in your household.

Many breeders recommend placing a piece of bedding from his former home in his new bed so that he recognises the scent of his littermates. Others still advise placing a hot water bottle in his bed for warmth. This latter may be a good idea provided the pup doesn't attempt to suckle—he'll get good and wet and may not fall asleep so fast.

Puppy's first night can be somewhat stressful for the pup and his new family. Remember that you are setting the tone of night-time at your house. Unless you want to play with your pup every evening at 10 p.m., midnight and 2 a.m., don't initiate the habit. Your family will thank you, and so will your pup!

TOXIC PLANTS

Many plants can be toxic to dogs. If you see your dog carrying a piece of vegetation in his mouth, approach him in a quiet, disinterested manner, avoid eye contact, pet him and gradually remove the plant from his mouth. Alternatively, offer him a treat and maybe he'll drop the plant on his own accord. Be sure no toxic plants are growing in your own garden.

PREVENTING PUPPY PROBLEMS

SOCIALISATION

Now that you have done all of the preparatory work and have helped your pup get accustomed to his new home and family, it is about time for you to have some fun! Socialising your Clumber Spaniel pup gives you the opportunity to show off your new friend, and your pup gets to reap the benefits of being an adorable furry creature that people will want to pet and, in general, think is absolutely precious!

Besides getting to know his new family, your puppy should be exposed to other people, animals and situations, but of course he must not come into close contact with dogs you don't know well until his course of injections is fully complete. This will help him become well adjusted as he grows up and less prone to being timid or fearful of the new things he will encounter. Your pup's socialisation began at the breeder's but now it is your responsibility to

SOCIALISATION

Thorough socialisation includes not only meeting new people but also being introduced to new experiences

such as riding in the car, having his coat brushed, hearing the television, walking in a crowd—the list is endless. The more your pup experiences, and the more positive the experiences are, the less of a shock and the less scary it will be for your pup to encounter new things.

continue it. The socialisation he receives up until the age of 12 weeks is the most critical, as this is the time when he forms his impressions of the outside world. Be especially careful during the eight-to-ten-week period, also known as the fear period. The interaction he receives during this time should be gentle and reassuring. Lack of socialisation can manifest itself in fear and aggression as the dog grows up. He needs lots of human contact, affection, handling and exposure to other animals.

Once your pup has received his necessary vaccinations, feel free to take him out and about (on his lead, of course). Walk him around the neighbourhood, take him on your daily errands, let people pet him, let him meet other dogs and pets, etc. Puppies do not have to try to make friends; there will be no shortage of people who will want to introduce themselves. Just make sure that you carefully supervise each meeting. If the neighbourhood children want to say hello, for example, that is great—children and pups most often make great companions. Sometimes an excited child can unintentionally handle a pup too roughly, or an overzealous pup can playfully nip a little too hard. You want to make socialisation

Fetch is an age-old game between man and dog. This young Clumber thrives on quality time with his owner.

experiences positive ones. What a pup learns during this very formative stage will impact his attitude toward future encounters. You want your dog to be comfortable around everyone. A pup that has a bad experience with a child may grow up to be a dog that is shy around or aggressive toward children.

Consistency in Training

Dogs, being pack animals, naturally need a leader, or else they try to establish dominance in their packs. When you bring a dog into your family, the choice of who becomes the leader and who becomes the 'pack' is entirely up to you! Your pup's intuitive quest for dominance, coupled with the fact that it is nearly impossible to look at an adorable Clumber Spaniel pup, with his 'puppy-dog' eyes, his fuzzy ears, and mischievous expression and not cave in, give the pup almost an unfair advantage in getting the upper hand! A pup will definitely test the waters to see what he can and cannot do. Do not give in to those pleading eyes—stand your ground

Clumbers are not the easiest dogs to train. Approach the training process with patience and persistence, and your Clumber will respond. Treats make training more interesting to the unresponsive Clumber.

While every puppy is unique, all puppies—especially Clumbers—have certain proclivities and habits that can be problematic if not stopped early on.

when it comes to disciplining the pup and make sure that all family members do the same. It will only confuse the pup when Mother tells him to get off the sofa when he is used to sitting up there with Father to watch the nightly news. Avoid discrepancies by having all members of the household decide on the rules before the pup even comes home...and be consistent in enforcing them! Early training shapes the dog's personality, so you cannot be unclear in what you expect.

COMMON PUPPY PROBLEMS

The best way to prevent puppy problems is to be proactive in stopping an undesirable behaviour as soon as it starts. The old saying 'You can't teach an old dog new tricks' does not necessarily hold true, but it is true that it is much easier to discourage bad behaviour in a young developing pup than to wait until the pup's bad behaviour becomes the adult dog's bad habit. There are some problems that are especially prevalent in puppies as they develop.

TRAINING TIP

Training your puppy takes much patience and can be frustrating at times, but you should see results from your efforts. If

you have a puppy that seems untrainable, take him to a trainer or behaviourist. The dog may have a personality problem that requires the help of a professional, or perhaps you need help in learning how to train your dog.

Nipping

As puppies start to teethe, they feel the need to sink their teeth into anything available...unfortunately that includes your fingers, arms, hair, and toes. You may find this behaviour cute for the first five seconds...until you feel just how sharp those puppy teeth are. This is something you want to discourage immediately and consistently with a firm 'No!' (or whatever number of firm 'No's' it takes for him to understand that you mean business). Then replace your finger with an appropriate chew toy. Whilst this behaviour is merely annoying when the dog is young, it can become dangerous as your Clumber Spaniel's adult teeth grow in and his jaws develop, and he continues to think it is okay to gnaw on human appendages.

Crying/Whining

Your pup will often cry, whine, whimper, howl or make some type of commotion when he is left alone. This is basically his way of calling out for attention to make sure that you know he is there and that you have not forgotten about him. He feels insecure when he is left alone, when you are out of the house and he is in his crate or when you are in another part of the house and he cannot see you. The noise he is making is an expression of the anxiety he feels at being alone, so

CHEWING TIPS

Chewing goes hand in hand with nipping in the sense that a teething puppy is always looking for a way to soothe his aching gums. In this case, instead of chewing on you, he may have taken a liking to your favourite shoe or something else which he should not be chewing. Again, realise that this is a normal canine behaviour that does not need to be discouraged, only redirected. Your pup just needs to be taught what is acceptable to chew on and what is off limits. Consistently tell him NO when you catch him chewing on something forbidden and give him a chew toy. Conversely, praise him when you catch him chewing on something appropriate. In this way you are discouraging the inappropriate behaviour and reinforcing the desired behaviour. The puppy chewing should stop after his adult teeth have come in, but an adult dog continues to chew for various reasons—perhaps because he is bored, perhaps to relieve tension or perhaps he just likes to chew. That is why it is important to redirect his chewing when he is still young.

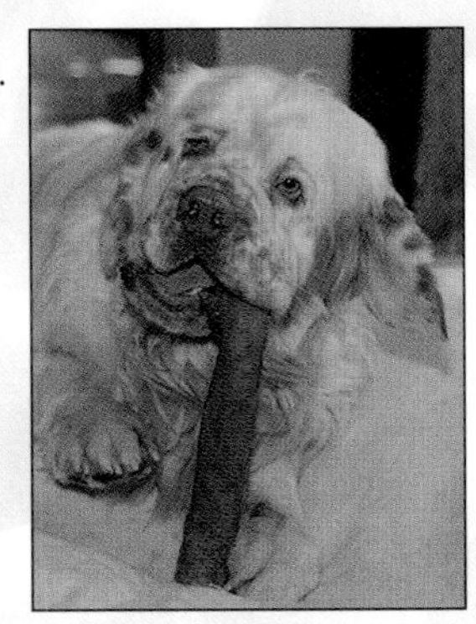

BOY OR GIRL?

An important consideration to be discussed is the sex of your puppy. For a family companion, a bitch may

be the better choice, considering the female's inbred concern for all young creatures and her accompanying tolerance and patience. It is always advisable to spay a pet bitch, which may guarantee her a longer life.

he needs to be taught that being alone is okay. You are not actually training the dog to stop making noise, you are training him to feel comfortable when he is alone and thus removing the need for him to make the noise. This is where the crate with cosy bedding and a toy comes in handy. You want to know that he is safe when you are not there to supervise, and you know that he will be safe in his crate rather than roaming freely about the house. In order for the pup to stay in his crate without making a fuss, he needs to be comfortable in his crate. On that note, it is extremely important that the crate is never used for punishment, or the pup will have a negative association with the crate.

Accustom the pup to the crate in short, gradually increasing time intervals in which you put him in the crate, maybe with a treat, and stay in the room with him. If he cries or makes a fuss, do not go to him, but stay in his sight. Gradually he will realise that staying in his crate is all right without your help, and it will not be so traumatic for him when you are not around. You may want to leave the radio on softly when you leave the house; the sound of human voices may be comforting to him.

DID YOU KNOW?

The majority of problems that is commonly seen in young pups will disappear as your dog gets older. However, how you deal with problems when he is young will determine how he

reacts to discipline as an adult dog. It is important to establish who is boss (hopefully it will be you!) right away when you are first bonding with your dog. This bond will set the tone for the rest of your life together.

EVERYDAY CARE OF YOUR

CLUMBER SPANIEL

DIETARY AND FEEDING CONSIDERATIONS

Today the choices of food for your Clumber Spaniel are many and varied. There are simply dozens of brands of food in all sorts of flavours and textures, ranging from puppy diets to those for seniors. There are even hypoallergenic and low-calorie diets available. Because your Clumber Spaniel's food has a bearing on coat, health and temperament, it is essential that the most suitable diet be selected for a Clumber Spaniel of his age. It is fair to say, however, that even dedicated owners can be somewhat perplexed by the enormous range of foods available. Only understanding what is best for your dog will help you reach a valued decision.

Dog foods are produced in three basic types: dried, semi-moist and tinned. Dried foods are useful for the cost-conscious for overall they tend to be less expensive than semi-moist or tinned. These contain the least fat and the most preservatives. In general, tinned foods are made up of 60–70 percent water, whilst semi-moist ones often contain so much sugar that they are perhaps the least preferred by owners, even though their dogs seem to like them.

When selecting your dog's diet, three stages of development must be considered: the puppy stage, adult stage and the senior or veteran stage.

PUPPY STAGE

Puppies instinctively want to suck milk from their mother's teats and a normal puppy will exhibit this behaviour from just a few moments following birth. If puppies do not attempt to suckle within the first half-hour or so, they should be encouraged to do so by placing them on a nipple,

DID YOU KNOW?

A good test for proper diet is the colour, odour and firmness of your dog's stool. A healthy dog usually produces three semi-hard stools per day. The stools should have no unpleasant odour. They should be the same colour from excretion to excretion.

Puppies should be allowed to nurse for three to four entire weeks before the breeder initiates the weaning process.

having selected one with plenty of milk. This early milk supply is important in providing colostrum to protect the puppies during the first eight to ten weeks of their lives. Although a mother's milk is much better than any milk formula, despite there being some excellent ones available, if the puppies do not feed, the breeder has to feed them himself. For those with less experience, advice from a veterinary surgeon is important so that you feed the correct quality and right quantity of milk at suitably frequent intervals, usually every two hours during the first few days of life.

Puppies should be allowed to nurse for three to four weeks and should be slowly weaned away from their mother by introducing small portions of raw chopped meat, cereal and tinned milk. By

DID YOU KNOW?

Dog food must be at room temperature, neither too hot nor too cold. Fresh water, changed daily and served in a clean bowl, is mandatory, especially when feeding dried food.

Never feed your dog from the table while you are eating. Never feed your dog left-overs from your own meal. They usually contain too much fat and too much seasoning.

Dogs must chew their food. Hard pellets are excellent; soups and slurries are to be avoided.

Don't add left-overs or any extras to normal dog food. The normal food is usually balanced and adding something extra destroys the balance.

Except for age-related changes, dogs do not require dietary variations. They can be fed the same diet, day after day, without their becoming ill.

the time they are six weeks old, they should be completely weaned and fed solely a puppy dried food. In the beginning you should always soak the dried food in boiling water so that it is soft enough for the puppy to eat until it gets its teeth. During this weaning period the diet is most important, as the puppy grows fastest during its first year of life. It has been determined by experienced and knowledgeable Clumber Spaniel breeders that puppy food should not be given after three to four months of age because it encourages the heavier breeds to grow too quickly. It is strongly recommended that adult food be started at this time. The dog will attain its proper size, but at a slower, healthier rate. Some breeders do not give puppy food at all.

Puppy diets should be balanced for your dog's needs and supplements of vitamins, minerals and protein should not be necessary and can even be dangerous. Puppies up to eight

DID YOU KNOW?

You must store your dried dog food carefully. Open packages of dog food quickly lose their vitamin value, usually within 90 days of being opened. Mould spores and vermin could also contaminate the food.

FOOD PREFERENCE

Selecting the best dried dog food is difficult. There is no majority consensus amongst veterinary scientists as to the value of nutrient analyses (protein, fat, fibre, moisture, ash, cholesterol, minerals, etc.). All agree that feeding trials are what matters, but you also have to consider the individual dog. Its weight, age, activity and what

pleases its taste, all must be considered. It is probably best to take the advice of your veterinary surgeon. Every dog's dietary requirements vary, even during the lifetime of a particular dog.

If your dog is fed a good dried food, it does not require supplements of meat or vegetables. Dogs do appreciate a little variety in their diets so you may choose to stay with the same brand, but vary the flavour. Alternatively you may wish to add a little flavoured stock to give a difference to the taste.

weeks of age should be fed four times a day, then three times a day until four to six months and then twice a day throughout their lives. Some dog people do feed adult dogs once a day but it is healthier to divide the food into two meals, if you have the extra time to devote to this.

Fit, active Clumbers will require a different diet than dogs that are less frequently exercised.

GRAIN-BASED DIETS

Some less expensive dog foods are based on grains and other plant proteins. Whilst these products may appear to be attractively priced, many breeders prefer a diet based on animal proteins and believe that they are more conducive to your dog's health. Many grain-based diets rely on soy protein that may cause flatulence (passing gas).

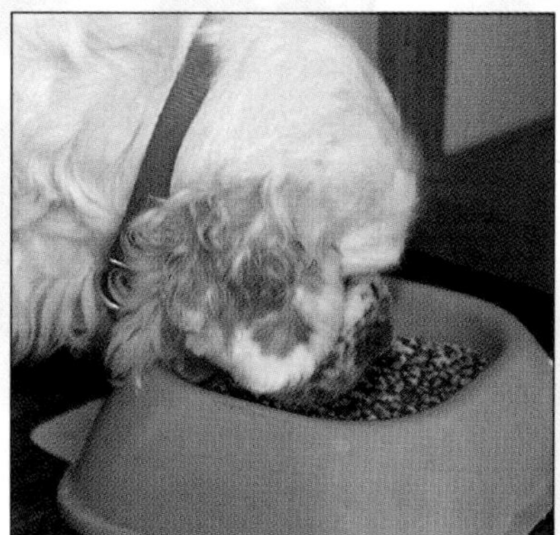

There are many cases, however, when your dog might require a special diet. These special requirements should only be recommended by your veterinary surgeon.

Adult Diets

A dog is considered an adult when it has stopped growing. A Clumber Spaniel reaches adulthood at about two years of age whilst other breeds may take up to three years. Again you should rely upon your veterinary surgeon or dietary specialist to recommend an acceptable maintenance diet. Major dog food manufacturers specialise in this type of food, and it is merely necessary for you to select the one best suited to your dog's needs. Active dogs may have different requirements than sedate dogs.

Senior Diets

As dogs get older, their metabolism changes. The older dog usually exercises less, moves more slowly and sleeps more. This change in lifestyle and physiological performance requires a change in diet. Since these changes take place slowly, they might not be recognisable. What is easily recognisable is weight gain. By continuing to feed

What are you feeding your dog?

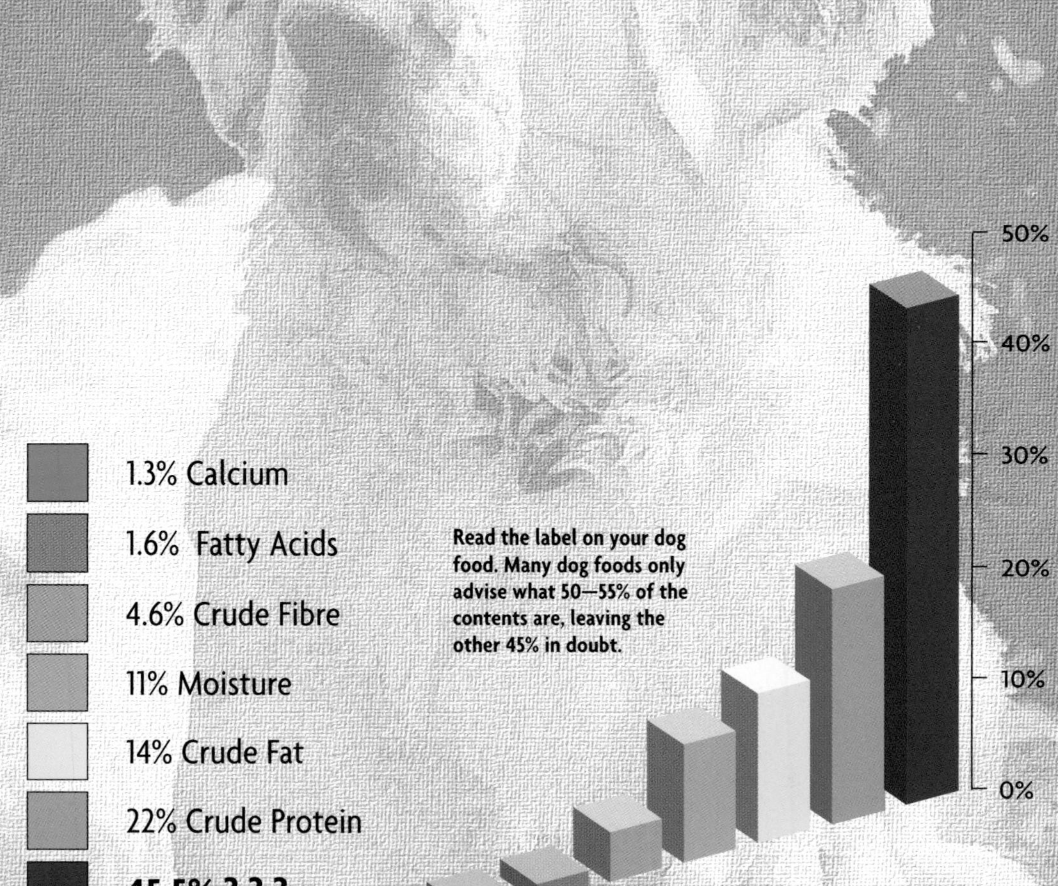

your dog an adult-maintenance diet when it is slowing down metabolically, your dog will gain weight. Obesity in an older dog compounds the health problems that already accompany old age.

As your dog gets older, few of his organs function up to par. The kidneys slow down and the intestines become less efficient. These age-related factors are best handled with a change in diet and a change in feeding schedule to give smaller portions that are more easily digested.

Daily walks with your Clumber Spaniel are excellent exercise for dog and master alike. Walking the dog on the pavement reliably wears down the dog's nails, reducing the need for trimming.

There is no single best diet for every older dog. Whilst many dogs do well on light or senior diets, other dogs do better on puppy diets or other special premium diets such as lamb and rice. Your vet may suggest a specific diet to help control an age-related problem. Be sensitive to your senior Clumber Spaniel's diet and this will help control other problems that may arise with your old friend.

WATER

Just as your dog needs proper nutrition from his food, water is an essential 'nutrient' as well. Water keeps the dog's body properly hydrated and promotes normal function of the body's systems. Make sure that the dog's water bowl is clean, and change the water often, making sure that water is always available for your dog, especially if you feed dried food.

EXERCISE

All dogs require some form of exercise regardless of breed and a sedentary lifestyle is as harmful to a dog as it is to a person. The Clumber Spaniel is a moderately active dog. Whilst it seems that a Clumber would rather lie on the sofa, regular walks, play sessions in the garden, or letting the dog run free in the garden under your supervision are necessary forms of exercise for him. For those who are more ambitious, you will find that your Clumber Spaniel also enjoys long walks, an occasional hike or even a swim! Bear in mind that an overweight dog should never be suddenly over-exercised; instead he should be allowed to increase exercise slowly. Not only is exercise essential to keep the dog's body fit, it is essential to his mental well being. A bored dog will find something to do, which often manifests itself in some type of destructive behaviour. In this sense, it is essential for the owner's mental well being as well!

DID YOU KNOW?

You should be careful where you exercise your dog. Many countryside areas have been sprayed with chemicals that are highly toxic to both dogs and humans. Never allow your dog to eat grass or drink from puddles on either public or private grounds, as the run-off water may contain chemicals from sprays and herbicides.

GROOMING

Brushing

Clumber Spaniels do not require extensive grooming, as they are considered a natural dog. A pin brush or a metal rake can be used for routine brushing. Brush the coat several times a week to remove dead hair and stimulate the dog's natural oils, adding shine and a healthy look to the coat. Clumber Spaniels should never have the neck shaved as some spaniels do. Their feet should be tidied and the hair in their pads should be trimmed. You should check that there are no stones or mats between the pads of their feet to hinder their walking. You may also want to trim the hair under their ears as that is the first place that mats. Under their front elbows is another place that mats easily. You should also check the hair above their hocks as it often mats and make sure there are no faeces stuck under the tail. Brush more in those places where the hair is the longest. Regular grooming sessions are also a good way to spend time with your dog. Many dogs grow to like the feel of being brushed and will enjoy the routine.

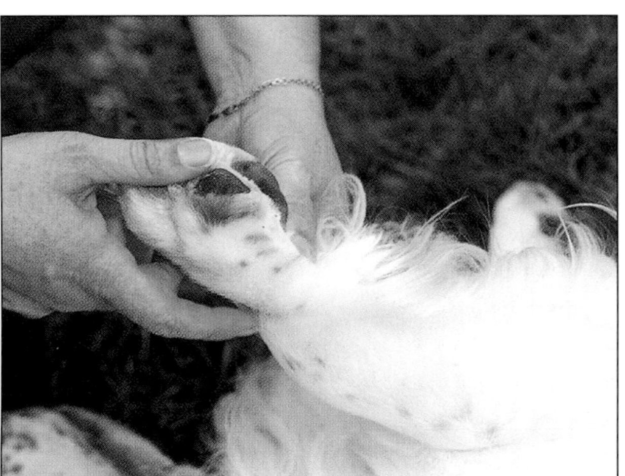

Check between your Clumber's pads for any debris or stones that may accumulate there.

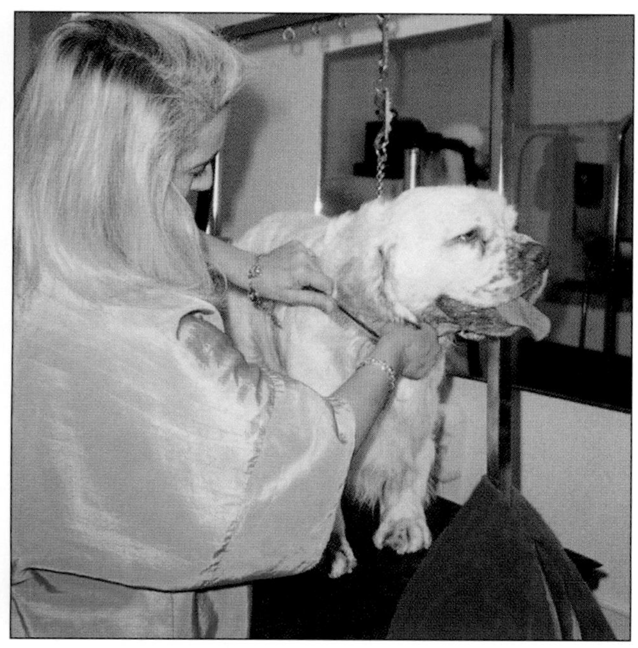

BATHING TIP

The use of human soap products like shampoo, bubble bath and hand soap can be damaging to a dog's coat and skin. Human products are too strong and remove the protective oils coating the dog's hair and skin (making him water-resistant). Use only shampoo made especially for dogs and you may like to use a medicated shampoo, which will always help to keep external parasites at bay.

You can easily groom your own Clumber Spaniel, but if you prefer, professional assistance is usually available close to your home.

Regular grooming and bathing will keep your Clumber looking and smelling clean. Brushing reduces the clumps of Clumber fur that will be found on your furniture.

Bathing

Dogs do not need to be bathed as often as humans, but regular bathing is essential for healthy skin and a healthy, shiny coat. Again, like most anything, if you accustom your pup to being bathed as a puppy, it will be second nature by the time he grows up. You want your dog to be at ease in the bath or else it could end up a wet, soapy, messy ordeal for both of you!

Brush your Clumber Spaniel thoroughly before wetting his coat. This will minimise tangles and mats, get rid of dust and dandruff, and remove any dead hair. The feathers should be combed out to make sure there are no mats. Make sure that your dog has a good non-slip surface to stand on. Begin by wetting the dog's coat. A shower or hose attachment is necessary for thoroughly wetting and rinsing the coat. Check the water temperature to make sure that it is neither too hot nor too cold.

Next, apply shampoo to the dog's coat and work it into a good lather. You should purchase a shampoo that is made for dogs. Do not use a product made for human

hair. Wash the head last; you do not want shampoo to drip into the dog's eyes whilst you are washing the rest of his body. Work the shampoo all the way down to the skin. You can use this opportunity to check the skin for any bumps, bites or other abnormalities. Do not neglect any area of the body—get all of the hard-to-reach places.

Once the dog has been thoroughly shampooed, he requires an equally thorough rinsing. Shampoo left in the coat can be irritating to the skin. Protect his eyes from the shampoo by shielding them with your hand and directing the flow of water in the opposite direction. You should also avoid getting water in

BATHING TIP

Once you are sure that the dog is thoroughly rinsed, squeeze the excess water out of the coat with your hand and dry him with a heavy towel. You may choose to use a blaster on his coat or just let it dry naturally. In cold weather, never allow your dog outside with a wet coat.

There are 'dry bath' products on the market, which are sprays and powders intended for spot cleaning, that can be used between regular baths, if necessary. They are not substitutes for regular baths, but they are easy to use for touch-ups as they do not require rinsing.

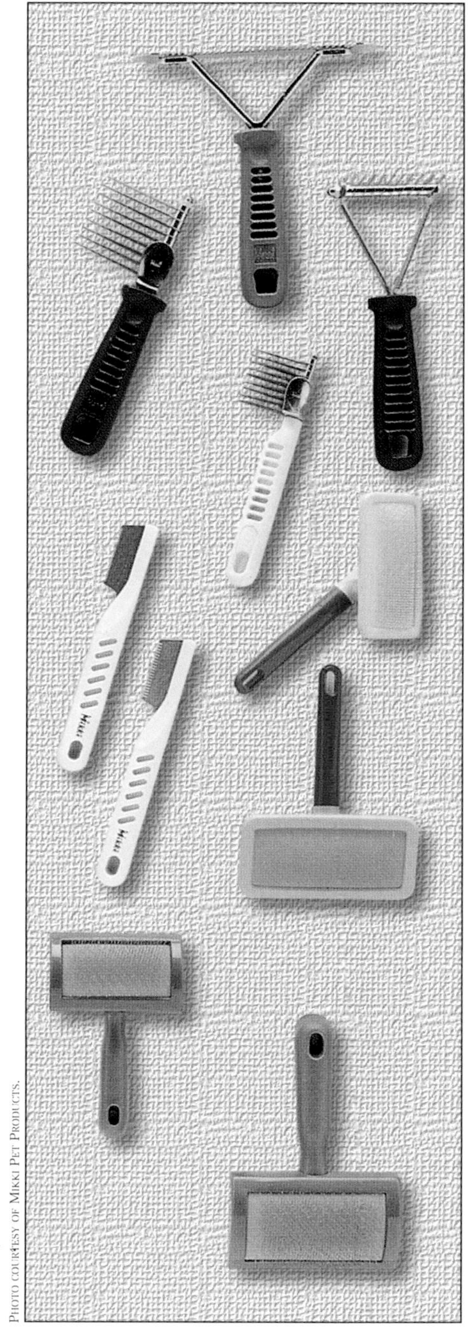

Photo courtesy of Mikki Pet Products.

Suitable brushes and combs are available at your local pet shop.

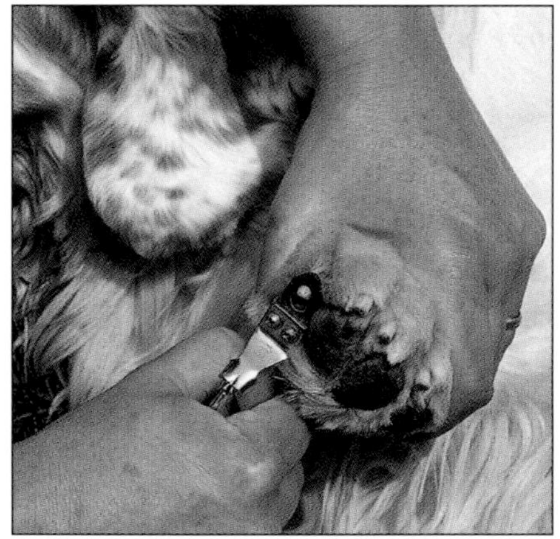

Use a guillotine-style nail clipper to trim your Clumber's nails. These can be purchased at your pet shop.

the ear canal. You should use a dog coat conditioner after the soap has been rinsed away. Using conditioner at the end of the bath not only helps remove tangles but also helps to prevent them. Be prepared for your dog to shake out his coat—you might want to stand back, but make sure you have a hold on the dog to keep him from running through the house.

Ear Cleaning

The ears should be kept clean and any excess hair inside the ear should be carefully cut. Ears can be cleaned with a cotton wipe and special cleaner or ear powder made especially for dogs. Be on the lookout for any signs of infection or ear mite infestation. If your Clumber Spaniel has been shaking his head or scratching at his ears frequently, this usually indicates a problem. If his ears have an unusual odour, this is a sure sign of mite infestation or infection, and a signal to have his ears checked by the veterinary surgeon.

Nail Clipping

Your Clumber Spaniel should be accustomed to having his nails trimmed at an early age, since it will be part of your maintenance routine throughout his life. Not only does it look nicer but long nails can be sharp if they scratch someone unintentionally. Also, a long nail has a better chance of ripping and bleeding, or causing the feet to spread. A good rule of thumb is that if you can hear your dog's nails clicking on the floor when he walks, his nails are too long.

GROOMING EQUIPMENT

How much grooming equipment you purchase will depend on how much grooming you are going to do. Here are some basics:

- Natural bristle brush
- Slicker brush
- Metal comb
- Scissors
- Blaster
- Rubber mat
- Dog shampoo
- Spray hose attachment
- Ear cleaner
- Cotton wipes
- Towels
- Nail clippers

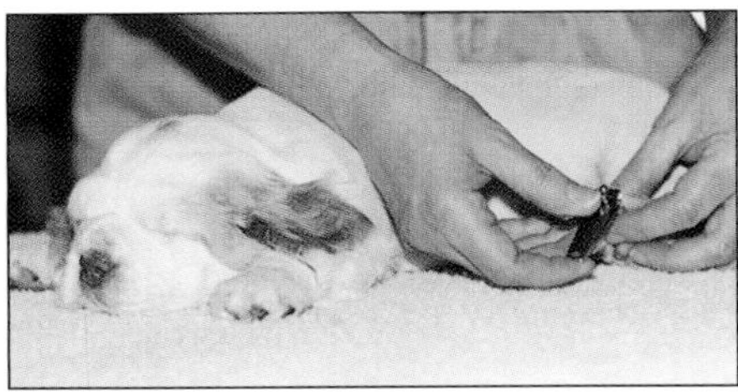

Before you start cutting, make sure you can identify the 'quick' in each nail. The quick is a blood vessel that runs through the centre of each nail and grows rather close to the end. It will bleed if accidentally cut, which will be quite painful for the dog, as it contains nerve endings. Keep some type of clotting agent on hand, such as a styptic pencil or styptic powder (the type used for shaving). This will stop the bleeding quickly when applied to the end of the cut nail. Do not panic if this happens, just stop the bleeding and talk soothingly to your dog. Once he has calmed down, move on to the next nail. It is better to clip a little at a time, particularly with black-nailed dogs.

Hold your pup steady as you begin trimming his nails; you do not want him to make any sudden movements or run away. Talk to him soothingly and stroke him as you clip. Holding his foot in your hand, simply take off the end of each nail in one quick clip. If your dog has dew claws, do not forget to clip them as they can grow around and into the leg. You

Nail Maintenance

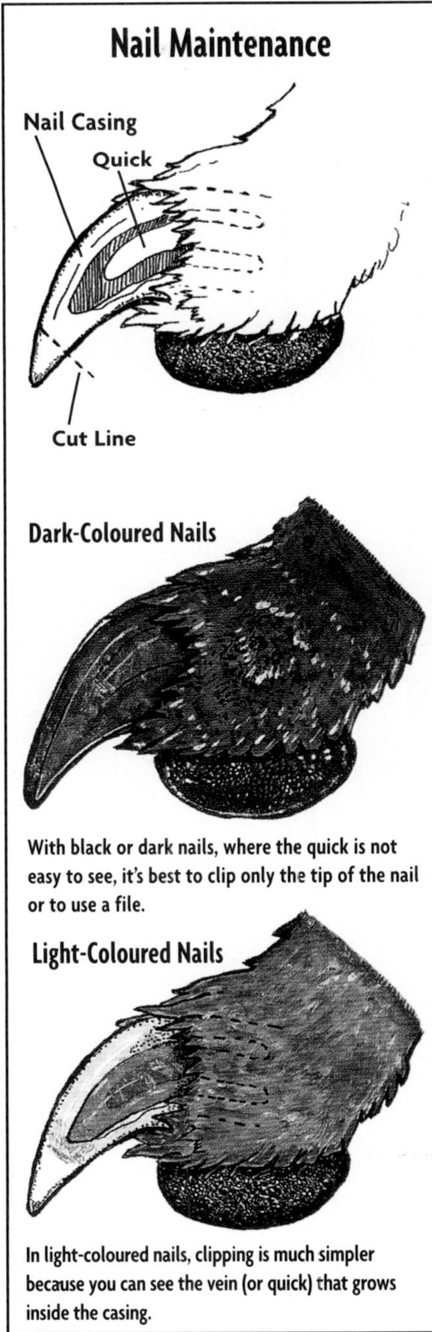

With black or dark nails, where the quick is not easy to see, it's best to clip only the tip of the nail or to use a file.

In light-coloured nails, clipping is much simpler because you can see the vein (or quick) that grows inside the casing.

For a very small puppy, you can utilise a nail clipper designed for human use, but once the pup grows up a dog clipper will be necessary.

DID YOU KNOW?

A dog that spends a lot of time outside on a hard surface, such as cement or pavement, will have his nails naturally worn down and may not need to have them trimmed as often, except maybe in the colder months when he is not

outside as much. Regardless, it is best to get your dog accustomed to this procedure at an early age so that he is used to it. Some dogs are especially sensitive about having their feet touched, but if a dog has experienced it since he was young, he should not be bothered by it.

can purchase nail clippers that are specially made for dogs; you can probably find them wherever you buy pet or grooming supplies.

TRAVELLING WITH YOUR DOG

Car Travel

You should accustom your Clumber Spaniel to riding in a car at an early age. You may or may not take him in the car often, but at the very least he will need to go to the vet and you do not want these trips to be traumatic for the dog or problematic for you. The safest way for a dog to ride in the car is in his crate. If he uses a crate in the house, you can use the same crate for travel. Whilst fibreglass crates are used for aeroplane travel, a dog enjoys the added viewing from a wire crate in the car. Put the pup in the crate and see how he reacts. If he seems uneasy, you can have a passenger hold him on his lap whilst you drive. Of course, this solution will only work when your Clumber is

TRAVEL TIP

Never leave your dog alone in the car. In hot weather your dog can die from the high temperature inside a closed vehicle; even a car parked in the shade can heat up very quickly. Leaving the window open is dangerous as well since the dog can hurt himself trying to get out.

a puppy! Another option is a specially made safety harness for dogs, which straps the dog in much like a seat belt. Do not let the dog roam loose in the vehicle—this is very dangerous! If you should stop short, your dog can be thrown and injured. If the dog starts climbing on you and pestering you whilst you are driving, you will not be able to concentrate on the road. It is an unsafe situation for everyone—human and canine.

For long trips, be prepared to stop to let the dog relieve himself. Bring along whatever you need to clean up after him. You should take along some paper kitchen towels and perhaps some old towelling for use should he have an accident in the car or suffer from travel sickness.

Air Travel

Whilst it is possible to take a dog on a flight within Britain, this is fairly unusual and advance

You must use a crate for transporting your Clumber. They should not be allowed loose within a moving vehicle. Crate training pays off for travelling as well as housebreaking.

permission is always required. The dog will be required to travel in a fibreglass crate and you should always check in advance with the airline regarding specific requirements. To help the dog be at ease, put one of his favourite toys in the crate with him. Do not feed the dog for at least six hours before the trip to minimise his need to relieve himself. However, certain regulations specify that water must always be made available to the dog in the crate.

Make sure your dog is properly identified and that your contact information appears on his ID tags and on his crate. Animals travel in a different area of the plane than human passengers so every rule must be strictly adhered to so as to prevent the risk of getting separated from your dog.

TRAVEL TIP

For international travel you will have to make arrangements well in advance (perhaps months), as countries' regulations pertaining to bringing in animals differ. There may be special health certificates and/or vaccinations that your dog will need before taking the trip; sometimes this has to be done within a certain time frame. In rabies-free countries, you will need to bring proof of the dog's rabies vaccination and there may be a quarantine period upon arrival.

TRAVEL TIP

If you are going on a long motor trip with your dog, be sure the hotels are dog friendly. Many hotels do not accept dogs. Also take along some ice that can be thawed and offered to your dog if he becomes overheated. Most dogs like to lick ice.

BOARDING

So you want to take a family holiday—and you want to include *all* members of the family. You would probably make arrangements for accommodations ahead of time anyway, but this is especially important when travelling with a dog. You do not want to make an overnight stop at the only place around for miles and find out that they do not allow dogs. Also, you do not want to reserve a place for your family without confirming that you are travelling with a dog because if it is against their policy to allow dogs, you may not have a place to stay.

Alternatively, if you are travelling and choose not to take your Clumber Spaniel, you will have to make arrangements for him whilst you are away. Some options are to take him to a neighbour's house to stay, to have a trusted neighbour pop in often or stay at your house or bring your dog to a reputable

Many breeders offer boarding facilities. If your breeder lives close to your home, this may be a viable option when you're planning a holiday.

TRAVEL TIP

When travelling, never let your dog off-lead in a strange area. Your dog could run away out of fear or decide

to chase a passing squirrel or cat or simply want to stretch his legs without restriction—you might never see your canine friend again.

boarding kennel.

If you choose to board him at a kennel, you should visit in advance to see the facility provided, how clean it is and where the dogs are kept. Talk to some of the employees and see how they treat the dogs—do they spend time with the dogs, play with them, exercise them, etc.? Also find out the kennel's policy on vaccinations and what they require. This is for all of the dogs' safety, since there is a greater risk of diseases being passed from dog to dog when they are kept together.

IDENTIFICATION

Your Clumber Spaniel is your valued companion and friend. That is why you always keep a close eye on him and you have made sure that he cannot escape from the garden or wriggle out of his collar and run away from you. However, accidents can happen and there may come a time when your dog unexpectedly gets separated from you. If this unfortunate event should occur, the first thing on your mind will be finding him. Proper identification will increase the chances of his being returned to you safely and quickly. One method of identification is a tattoo either on the inside of the ear or on the inside of a rear leg. Often these are hard to find and may fade as the dog grows. The newest and most successful method of identification is the microchip. This works extremely well if the person or group finding the dog has a scanner and the dog is registered with a central organisation. This is gaining in use in England and the United States and has helped many lost dogs to be reunited with their owners.

TRAVEL TIP

The most extensive travel you do with your dog may be limited to trips to the veterinary surgeon's office—or you may decide to bring him along for long distances when the family goes on holiday. Whichever the case, it is important to consider your dog's safety while travelling.

ID SECURITY

As puppies become more and more expensive, especially those puppies of high quality for showing and/or breeding, they have a greater chance of being stolen. The usual collar dog tag is, of course, easily removed. But there are two techniques that have become widely used for identification.

The puppy microchip implantation involves the injection of a small microchip, about the size of a corn kernel, under the skin of the dog. If your dog shows up at a clinic or shelter, or is offered for resale under less than savory circumstances, it can be positively identified by the microchip. The microchip is scanned and a registry quickly identifies you as the owner. This is not only protection against theft, but should the dog run away or go chasing a squirrel and get lost, you have a fair chance of getting it back.

Tattooing is done on various parts of the dog, from its belly to its cheeks. The number tattooed can be your telephone number or any other number which you can easily memorise. When professional dog thieves see a tattooed dog, they usually lose interest in it. Both microchipping and tattooing can be done at your local veterinary clinic. For the safety of our dogs, no laboratory facility or dog broker will accept a tattooed dog as stock.

HOUSEBREAKING AND TRAINING YOUR CLUMBER SPANIEL

Living with an untrained dog is a lot like owning a piano that you do not know how to play—it is a nice object to look at but it does not do much more than that to bring you pleasure. Now try taking piano lessons and suddenly the piano comes alive and brings forth magical sounds and rhythms that set your heart singing and your body swaying.

The same is true with your Clumber Spaniel. Any dog is a big responsibility and if not trained sensibly may develop unacceptable behaviour that annoys you or could even cause family friction. A dog that develops unacceptable behaviour from lack of socialisation or lack of training often ends up in the pound. This can be avoided by communication with your dog and time committed to its proper training.

To train your Clumber Spaniel, you may like to enrol in an obedience class. Teach him good manners as you learn how and why he behaves the way he does. Find out how to communicate with your dog and how to recognise and understand his communications with you.

IDENTIFICATION

If your dog gets lost, he is not able to ask for directions home.

Identification tags fastened to the collar give important information—the dog's name, the owner's name, the owner's address and a telephone number where the owner can be reached. This makes it easy for whomever finds the dog to

contact the owner and arrange to have the dog returned. An added advantage is that a person will be more likely to approach a lost dog who has ID tags on his collar; it tells the person that this is somebody's pet rather than a stray. This is the easiest and fastest method of identification provided that the tags stay on the collar and the collar stays on the dog.

Suddenly the dog takes on a new role in your life—he is clever, interesting, well behaved and fun to be with. He demonstrates his bond of devotion to you daily. In other words, your Clumber Spaniel does wonders for your ego because he constantly reminds you that you are not only his leader, you are his hero!

DID YOU KNOW?

If you start with a normal, healthy dog and give him time, patience and some carefully executed lessons, you will reap the rewards of that training

for the life of the dog. And what a life it will be! The two of you will find immeasurable pleasure in the companionship you have built together with love, respect and understanding.

Those involved with teaching dog obedience and counselling owners about their dogs' behaviour have discovered some interesting facts about dog ownership. For example, training dogs when they are puppies (starting at four months although housetraining should begin at about three months) results in the highest rate of success in developing well-mannered and well-adjusted adult dogs. Training an older dog, from six months to six years of age, can produce almost equal results providing that the owner accepts the dog's slower rate of learning capability and is willing to work patiently to help the dog succeed at developing to his fullest potential. Unfortunately, many owners of untrained adult dogs lack the patience factor, so they do not persist until their dogs are successful at learning particular behaviours.

Training a puppy, aged 10 to 16 weeks (20 weeks at the most), is like working with a dry sponge in a pool of water. The pup soaks up whatever you show him and constantly looks for more things to do and learn. At this early age, his body is not yet producing hormones, and therein lies the reason for such a high rate of success. Without hormones, he is focused on his owners and not particularly interested in investigating other places, dogs, people, etc. You are his leader: his provider of food, water, shelter and security. He latches onto you and wants to stay close. He will usually follow you from room to room, will not let you out of his sight when you are outdoors with him, and respond in like manner to the people and animals you encounter. If you greet a friend warmly, he will be happy to greet the person as well. If, however, you are hesitant, even anxious, about the approach of a stranger, he will respond accordingly.

Once the puppy begins to produce hormones, his natural curiosity emerges and he begins to investigate the world around him. It is at this time when you may notice that the untrained dog begins to wander away from you and even ignore your commands to stay close.

There are usually classes within a reasonable distance of the owner's home, but you may also do a lot to train your dog yourself. Sometimes there are classes available but the tuition is too costly. Whatever the circumstances, the solution to the problem of lack of lesson availability lies within the pages of this book.

This chapter is devoted to helping you train your Clumber Spaniel at home. If the recommended procedures are followed faithfully, you may expect positive results that will prove rewarding to both you and your dog.

Whether your new charge is a puppy or a mature adult, the methods of teaching and the techniques we use in training basic behaviours are the same. After all, no dog, whether puppy or adult, likes harsh or inhumane methods. All creatures, however, respond favourably to gentle motivational methods and sincere praise and encouragement. Now let us get started.

DID YOU KNOW?

Training a dog is a life experience. Many parents admit that much of what they know about raising children they learned from caring for their dogs. Dogs respond to love, fairness and guidance, just as children do. Become a good dog owner and you may become an even better parent.

HELPING PAWS

Your dog may not be the next Lassie, but every pet has the potential to do some tricks well. Identify his natural talents and hone them. Is your dog always happy and upbeat? Teach him to wag his tail or give you his paw on command. Real homebodies can be trained to do household chores, such as carrying dirty washing or retrieving the morning paper.

HOUSEBREAKING

You can train a puppy to relieve itself wherever you choose, but this must be somewhere suitable. You should bear in mind from the outset that when your puppy is old enough to go out in public places, any canine deposits must be removed at once. You will always have to carry with you a small plastic bag or 'pooper-scooper.'

Outdoor training includes such surfaces as grass, mud or soil, earth and cement. When deciding on the surface and location that you will want your Clumber Spaniel to use, be sure it is going to be permanent. Training your dog to grass and then changing your mind two months later is extremely difficult for both dog and owner.

Next, choose the command you will use each and every time you want your puppy to void. 'Be quick,' "Hurry up' and 'Toilet' are examples of commands commonly used by dog owners.

Get in the habit of giving the puppy your chosen relief command before you take him out. That way, when he becomes an adult, you will be able to determine if he wants to go out when you ask him. A confirmation will be signs of interest, wagging his tail, watching you intently, going to the door, etc.

A pooper-scooper makes it more convenient to clean up after your dog.

DID YOU KNOW?

Dogs will do anything for your attention. If you reward the dog when he is calm and resting, you will develop a well-mannered dog. If, on

the other hand, you greet your dog excitedly and encourage him to wrestle and roughhouse with you, the dog will greet you the same way and you will have a hyper dog on your hands.

Puppy's Needs

Puppy needs to relieve himself after play periods, after each meal, after he has been sleeping and any time he indicates that he is looking for a place to urinate or defecate.

The urinary and intestinal tract muscles of very young puppies are not fully developed. Therefore, like human babies, puppies need to relieve themselves frequently.

Take your puppy out often—every hour for an eight-week-old, for example, and always immediately after sleeping and eating. The older the puppy, the less often he will need to relieve himself. Finally, as a mature healthy adult, he will require only three to five relief trips per day.

Housing

Since the types of housing and control you provide for your puppy has a direct relationship on the success of housetraining, we consider the various aspects of both before we begin training.

Bringing a new puppy home and turning him loose in your house can be compared to turning a child loose in a sports arena and telling the child that the place is all his! The sheer enormity of the place would be too much for him to handle.

Instead, offer the puppy clearly defined areas where he can play, sleep, eat and live. A room of the house where the family gathers is the most obvious choice. Puppies are social animals and need to feel a part of the pack

DID YOU KNOW?

Dogs are the most honourable animals in existence. They consider another species (humans) as their own. They interface with you. You

are their leader. Puppies perceive children to be on their level; their actions around small children are different from their behaviour around their adult masters.

THINK BEFORE YOU BARK!

Dogs are sensitive to their master's moods and emotions. Use your voice wisely when communicating with your dog. Never raise your voice at your dog unless you are angry and trying to correct him. 'Barking' at your dog can become as meaningless as 'dogspeak' is to you. Think before you bark!

CANINE DEVELOPMENT SCHEDULE

It is important to understand how and at what age a puppy develops into adulthood. If you are a puppy owner, consult the following Canine Development Schedule to determine the stage of development your puppy is currently experiencing. This knowledge will help you as you work with the puppy in the weeks and months ahead.

Period	Age	Characteristics
First to Third	Birth to Seven Weeks	Puppy needs food, sleep and warmth, and responds to simple and gentle touching. Needs mother for security and disciplining. Needs littermates for learning and interacting with other dogs. Pup learns to function within a pack and learns pack order of dominance. Begin socialising with adults and children for short periods. Begins to become aware of its environment.
Fourth	Eight to Twelve Weeks	Brain is fully developed. Needs socialising with outside world. Remove from mother and littermates. Needs to change from canine pack to human pack. Human dominance necessary. Fear period occurs between 8 and 16 weeks. Avoid fright and pain.
Fifth	Thirteen to Sixteen Weeks	Training and formal obedience should begin. Less association with other dogs, more with people, places, situations. Period will pass easily if you remember this is pup's change-to-adolescence time. Be firm and fair. Flight instinct prominent. Permissiveness and over-disciplining can do permanent damage. Praise for good behaviour.
Juvenile	Four to Eight Months	Another fear period about 7 to 8 months of age. It passes quickly, but be cautious of fright and pain. Sexual maturity reached. Dominant traits established. Dog should understand sit, down, come and stay by now.

Note: These are approximate time frames. Allow for individual differences in puppies.

right from the start. Hearing your voice, watching you whilst you are doing things and smelling you nearby are all positive reinforcers that he is now a member of your pack. Usually a family room, the kitchen or a nearby adjoining breakfast area is ideal for providing safety and security for both puppy and owner.

Within that room there should be a smaller area which the puppy can call his own. An alcove, a wire or fibreglass dog crate or a fenced (not boarded!) corner from which he can view the activities of his new family will be fine. The size of the area or crate is the key factor here. The area must be large enough for the puppy to lie down and stretch out as well as stand up without rubbing his head on the top, yet small enough so that he cannot relieve himself at one end and sleep at the other without coming into contact with his droppings until fully trained to

DID YOU KNOW?

To a dog's way of thinking, your hands are like his mouth in terms of a defence mechanism. If you squeeze him too tightly, he might just bite you because that would be his normal response. This is not aggressive biting and, although all biting should be discouraged, you need the discipline in learning how to handle your dog.

HOUSEBREAKING TIP

Never line your pup's sleeping area with newspaper. Puppy litters are usually raised on newspaper and, once in your home, the puppy will immediately associate newspaper with voiding. Never put newspaper on any floor while housetraining, as this will only confuse the puppy. If you are paper-training him, use paper in his designated relief area ONLY. Finally, restrict water intake after evening meals. Offer a few licks at a time—never let a young puppy gulp water after meals.

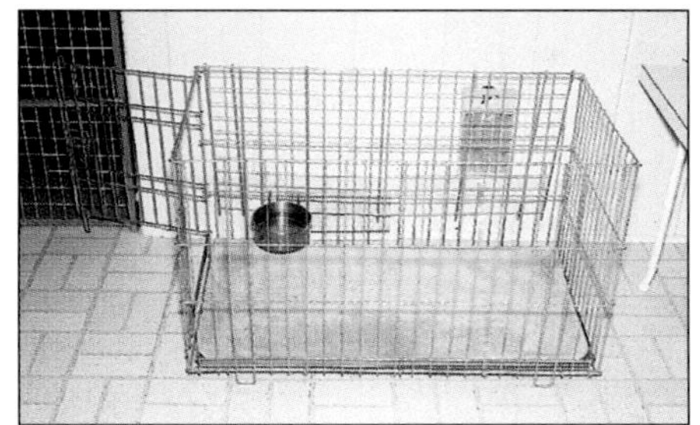

The wire crate must have a suitable water dish affixed to it so that the dog will not overturn it. Do not put water in your puppy's crate until he is completely housebroken.

TRAINING TIP

Your dog is actually training you at the same time you are training him.

Dogs do things to get attention. They usually repeat whatever succeeds in getting your attention

relieve himself outside.

Dogs are, by nature, clean animals and will not remain close to their relief areas unless forced to do so. In those cases, they then become dirty dogs and usually remain that way for life.

The crate or cubby should be lined with a clean towel (which may be chewed) and supplied with a toy or a raw marrowbone to chew on. Water must always be available, in a non-spill container.

Control

By control, we mean helping the puppy to create a lifestyle pattern that will be compatible to that of his human pack (YOU!). Just as we guide little children to learn our way of life, we must show the puppy when it is time to play, eat, sleep, exercise and even entertain himself.

Your puppy should always sleep in his crate. He should also learn that, during times of household confusion and excessive human activity such as at breakfast when family members are preparing for the day, he can play by himself in relative safety and comfort in his designated area. Each time you leave the puppy alone, he should understand exactly where he is to stay. You can gradually increase the time he is left alone to get him used to it.

Puppies are chewers. They cannot tell the difference between lamp cords, television wires, shoes, table legs, etc. Chewing into a television wire, for example, can be fatal to the puppy whilst a shorted wire can start a fire in the house. If the puppy

TONE OF VOICE

Most trainers suggest that an owner never use 'baby talk' with the dog. However, the tone of voice used in connection with that type of 'language' is almost always responded to in a positive way by any dog. Baby talk can be used at home for fun, but never should be used in training.

MEALTIME

Mealtime should be a peaceful time for your puppy. Do not put his food and water bowls in a high-traffic area in the house. For example, give him his own little corner of the kitchen where he can eat undisturbed and where he will not be under foot. Do not allow small children or other family members to disturb the pup when he is eating.

HOW MANY TIMES A DAY?

AGE	RELIEF TRIPS
To 14 weeks	10
14–22 weeks	8
22–32 weeks	6
Adulthood (dog stops growing)	4

These are estimates, of course, but they are a guide to the MINIMUM opportunities a dog should have each day to relieve itself.

chews on the arm of the chair when he is alone, you will probably discipline him angrily when you get home. Thus, he makes the association that your coming home means he is going to be punished. (He will not remember chewing the chair and is incapable of making the association of the discipline with his naughty deed.)

Other times of excitement, such as family parties, etc., can be fun for the puppy providing he can view the activities from the security of his designated area. He is not underfoot and he is not being fed all sorts of titbits that will probably cause him stomach distress, yet he still feels a part of the fun.

Schedule

A puppy should be taken to his relief area each time he is released from his designated area, after meals, after a play session, when he first awakens in the morning (at age eight weeks, this can mean 5 a.m.!). The puppy will indicate that he's ready 'to go' by circling

PRACTICE MAKES PERFECT!

- Have training lessons with your dog every day in several short segments—three to five times a day for a few minutes at a time is ideal.
- Do not have long practice sessions. The dog will become easily bored.
- Never practise when you are tired, ill, worried or in an otherwise negative mood. This will transmit to the dog and may have an adverse effect on its performance.

Think fun, short and above all POSITIVE! End each session on a high note, rather than a failed exercise, and make sure to give a lot of praise. Enjoy the training and help your dog enjoy it, too.

or sniffing busily—do not misinterpret these signs. For a puppy less than eight to ten weeks of age, a routine of taking him out every hour is necessary. As the puppy grows, he will be able to wait for longer periods of time.

Keep trips to his relief area short. Stay no more than five or six minutes and then return to the house. If he goes during that time, praise him lavishly and take him indoors immediately.

THE SUCCESS METHOD

Success that comes by luck is usually short lived. Success that comes by well-thought-out proven methods is often more easily achieved and permanent. This is the Success Method. It is designed to give you, the puppy owner, a simple yet proven way to help your puppy develop clean living habits and a feeling of security in his new environment.

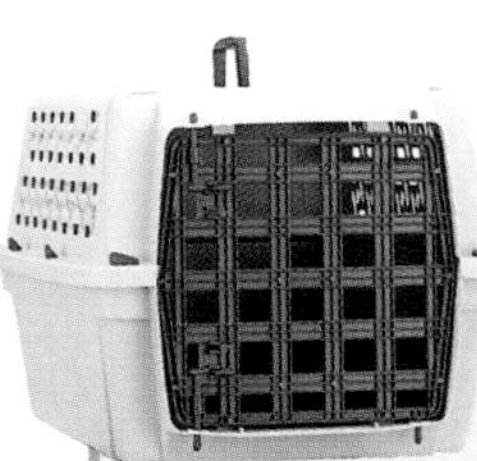

THE SUCCESS METHOD

1 Tell the puppy 'Crate time!' and place him in the crate with a small treat (a piece of cheese or half of a biscuit). Let him stay in the crate for five minutes while you are in the same room. Then release him and praise lavishly. Never release him when he is fussing. Wait until he is quiet before you let him out.

2 Repeat Step 1 several times a day.

3 The next day, place the puppy in the crate as before. Let him stay there for ten minutes. Do this several times.

4 Continue building time in five-minute increments until the puppy stays in his crate for 30 minutes with you in the room. Always take him to his relief area after prolonged periods in his crate.

5 Now go back to Step 1 and let the puppy stay in his crate for five minutes, this time while you are out of the room.

6 Once again, build crate time in five-minute increments with you out of the room. When the puppy will stay willingly in his crate (he may even fall asleep!) for 30 minutes with you out of the room, he will be ready to stay in it for several hours at a time.

6 Steps to Successful Crate Training

If he does not, but he has an accident when you go back indoors, pick him up immediately, say 'No! No!' and return to his relief area. Wait a few minutes, then return to the house again. Never hit a puppy or rub his face in urine or excrement when he has an accident!

Once indoors, put the puppy in his crate until you have had time to clean up his accident. Then release him to the family area and watch him more closely than before. Chances are, his accident was a result of your not picking up his signal or waiting too long before offering him the opportunity to relieve himself. Never hold a grudge against the puppy for accidents.

HOUSEBREAKING TIP

Most of all, be consistent. Always take your dog to the same location, always use the same command, and

always have him on lead when he is in his relief area, unless a fenced-in garden is available.

By following the Success Method, your puppy will be completely housetrained by the time his muscle and brain development reach maturity. Keep in mind that small breeds usually mature faster than large breeds, but all puppies should be trained by six months of age.

You should have the bare essentials for your Clumber puppy before the puppy arrives at your home. A crate, some toys, food, etc., are the bare necessities.

Let the puppy learn that going outdoors means it is time to relieve himself, not play. Once trained, he will be able to play indoors and out and still differentiate between the times for play versus the times for relief.

Help him develop regular hours for naps, being alone, playing by himself and just resting, all in his crate. Encourage him to entertain himself whilst you are busy with your activities. Let him learn that having you near is comforting, but it is not your main purpose in life to provide him with undivided attention.

Each time you put a puppy in his own area, use the same command, whatever suits best. Soon, he will run to his crate or special area when he hears you say those words. Crate training provides safety for you, the puppy and the home. It also provides the puppy with a feeling of security, and that helps the puppy achieve

THE GOLDEN RULE

The golden rule of dog training is simple. For each 'question' (command), there is only one correct answer (reaction). One command = one reaction. Keep practising the command until the dog reacts correctly without hesitating. Be repetitive but not monotonous. Dogs get bored just as people do!

Puppies are the easiest creatures on earth to bribe. A food treat does wonders to keep a puppy's attention, the perfect reward in every instance.

self-confidence and clean habits.

Remember that one of the primary ingredients in housetraining your puppy is control. Regardless of your lifestyle, there will always be occasions when you will need to have a place where your dog can stay and be happy and safe. However, you must remember that dogs get bored. They should be left in crates as short a time as possible (except during the night) and not because it is convenient for you to put him away. Later in life a dog may enjoy sleeping in its crate with the door open.

In conclusion, a few key elements are really all you need for a successful house training method—consistency, frequency, praise, control and supervision. By following these procedures with a normal, healthy puppy, you and the puppy will soon be past the stage of 'accidents' and ready to move on to a full and rewarding life together. Training is the answer for now and in the future.

ROLES OF DISCIPLINE, REWARD AND PUNISHMENT

Discipline, training one to act in accordance with rules, brings order to life. It is as simple as that. Without discipline, particularly in a group society, chaos reigns supreme and the group will eventually perish. Humans and canines are social animals and need some form of discipline in order to function effectively. They must procure food, protect their home base and their young and reproduce to keep the species going.

If there were no discipline in the lives of social animals, they would eventually die from starvation and/or predation by other stronger animals.

In the case of domestic canines, dogs need discipline in their lives in order to understand how their pack (you and other family members) functions and how they must act in order to survive.

A large humane society in a highly populated area recently surveyed dog owners regarding their satisfaction with their

HOUSEBREAKING TIP

By providing sleeping and resting quarters that fit the dog, and offering frequent opportunities to relieve himself outside his quarters, the puppy quickly learns that the outdoors (or the newspaper if you are training him to paper) is the place to go when he needs to urinate or defecate. It also reinforces his innate desire to keep his sleeping quarters clean. This, in turn, helps develop the muscle control that will eventually produce a dog with clean living habits.

relationships with their dogs. People who had trained their dogs were 75% more satisfied with their pets than those who had never trained their dogs.

Dr Edward Thorndike, a psychologist, established *Thorndike's Theory of Learning,* which states that a behaviour that results in a pleasant event tends to be repeated. A behaviour that results in an unpleasant event tends not to be repeated. It is this theory on which training methods are based today. For example, if you manipulate a dog to perform a specific behaviour and reward him for doing it, he is likely to do it again because he enjoyed the end result.

Occasionally, punishment, a penalty inflicted for an offence, is necessary. The best type of punishment often comes from an outside source. For example, a child is told not to touch the stove because he may get burned. He disobeys and touches the stove. In doing so, he receives a burn. From that time on, he respects the heat of the stove and avoids contact with it. Therefore, a behaviour that results in an unpleasant event tends not to be repeated.

A good example of a dog learning the hard way is the dog who chases the house cat. He is told many times to leave the cat alone, yet he persists in teasing the cat. Then, one day he begins chasing the cat but the cat turns and swipes a claw across the dog's face, leaving him with a painful gash on his nose. The final result is that the dog stops chasing the cat.

TRAINING TIP

Stand up straight and authoritatively when giving your dog commands. Do not issue commands when lying on the floor or lying on your back on the sofa. If you are on your hands and knees when you give a command, your dog will think you are positioning yourself to play.

DID YOU KNOW?

The puppy should also have regular play and exercise sessions when he is with you or a family member. Exercise for a very young puppy can consist of a short walk around the house or garden. Playing can include fetching games with a large ball or a special raggy. (All puppies teethe and need soft things upon which to chew.) Remember to restrict play periods to indoors within his living area (the family room, for example) until he is completely housetrained.

TRAINING EQUIPMENT

Collar and Lead

For a Clumber Spaniel the collar and lead that you use for training must be one with which you are

TRAINING TIP

Never call your dog to come to you for a correction or scold him when he reaches you. That is the quickest way to turn a 'Come' command into 'Go away fast!' Dogs think only in the present tense, and your dog will connect the scolding with coming to you, not with the misbehaviour of a few moments earlier.

easily able to work, not too heavy for the dog and perfectly safe. Most Clumber owners use a soft nylon slip collar. A chain choke collar wears away the neck hair and pinch or prong collars are never necessary for a Clumber Spaniel. *Remember to check the size of the collar as the dog grows so that it is not too tight.* A six-foot lead is used for training and can be used to walk your dog, but a flexi-lead is best for simply exercising your dog. Never use a chain lead as it is too heavy and not necessary for this breed.

Treats

Have a bag of treats on hand. Something nutritious and easy to swallow works best. Use a soft treat, a chunk of cheese or a piece of cooked chicken rather than a dry biscuit. By the time the dog has finished chewing a dry treat, he will forget why he is being rewarded in the first place! Using food rewards will not teach a dog to beg at the table—the only way to teach a dog to beg at the table is to give him food from the table. In training, rewarding the dog with a food treat will help him associate praise and the treats with learning new behaviours that obviously please his owner.

DID YOU KNOW?

If you want to be successful in training your dog, you have four rules to obey yourself:
1. Develop an understanding of how a dog thinks.
2. Do not blame the dog for lack of communication.

3. Define your dog's personality and act accordingly.
4. Have patience and be consistent.

Keeping training sessions enjoyable will convince your Clumber that he is having fun and wants to spend this structured time with you.

TRAINING BEGINS: ASK THE DOG A QUESTION

In order to teach your dog anything, you must first get his attention. After all, he cannot learn anything if he is looking away from you with his mind on something else.

To get his attention, ask him, 'School?' and immediately walk over to him and give him a treat as you tell him 'Good dog.' Wait a minute or two and repeat the routine, this time with a treat in your hand as you approach within a foot of the dog. Do not go directly to him, but stop about a foot short of him and hold out the treat as you ask, 'School?' He will see you approaching with a treat in your hand and most likely begin walking toward you. As you meet, give him the treat and praise again.

The third time, ask the question, have a treat in your hand and walk only a short distance toward the dog so that he must walk almost all the way to you. As he reaches you, give him the treat and praise again.

By this time, the dog will probably be getting the idea that if he pays attention to you, especially when you ask that question, it will pay off in treats and enjoyable activities for him. In other words, he learns that 'School' means doing exciting things with you that result in treats and positive attention for him.

Remember that the dog does not understand your verbal

DID YOU KNOW?

Dogs are as different from each other as people are. What works for one dog may not work for another.

Have an open mind. If one method of training is unsuccessful, try another.

language, he only recognises sounds. Your question translates to a series of sounds for him, and those sounds become the signal to go to you and pay attention; if he does, he will get to interact with you plus receive treats and praise.

THE BASIC COMMANDS

Teaching Sit

Now that you have the dog's attention, attach his lead and hold it in your left hand and a food treat in your right. Place your food hand at the dog's nose and let him lick the treat but not take it from you. Say 'Sit' and slowly raise your food hand from in front of the dog's nose up over his head so that he is looking at the ceiling. As he bends his head upward, he will have to bend his knees to maintain his balance. As he bends his knees, he will assume a sit position. At that point, release the food treat and praise lavishly with comments such as 'Good dog! Good sit!,' etc. Remember to always praise enthusiastically, because dogs relish verbal praise from their owners and feel so proud of themselves whenever they accomplish a behaviour.

Sit is the most basic command to teach your dog. This owner is working on obedience training her Clumber for competition.

TRAINING TIP

Dogs do not understand our language. They can be trained to react to a certain sound, at a certain volume. If you say 'No, Oliver' in a very soft pleasant voice it will not have the same meaning as 'No, Oliver!!' when you shout it as loud as you can. You should never use the dog's name during a reprimand, just the command NO!! Since dogs don't understand words, comics often use dogs trained with opposite meanings. Thus, when the comic commands his dog to SIT the dog will stand up, and vice versa.

Clumbers can be stubborn in learning the down. Never intimidate a dog to teach him the down. Forceful methods will produce no results with a Clumber Spaniel.

You will not use food forever in getting the dog to obey your commands. Food is only used to teach new behaviours, and once the dog knows what you want when you give a specific command, you will wean him off the food treats but still maintain the verbal praise. After all, you will always have your voice with you, and there will be many times when you have no food rewards but expect the dog to obey.

Teaching Down

Teaching the down exercise is easy when you understand how the dog perceives the down position, and it is very difficult when you do not. Dogs perceive the down position as a submissive one. Therefore teaching the down exercise using a forceful method can sometimes make the dog develop such a fear of the down that he either runs away when you say 'Down' or he attempts to snap at the person who tries to force him down.

Have the dog sit close alongside your left leg, facing in the same direction as you are. Hold the lead in your left hand and a food treat in your right. Now place your left hand lightly on the top of the dog's shoulders where they meet above the spinal cord. Do not push down on the dog's shoulders; simply rest your left hand there so you can guide the dog to lie down close to your left leg rather than to swing away from your side when he drops.

Now place the food hand at the dog's nose, say 'Down' very softly (almost a whisper), and slowly lower the food hand to the dog's front feet. When the food hand reaches the floor, begin moving it forward along the floor in front of the dog. Keep talking softly to the dog, saying things like, 'Do you want this treat? You can do this, good dog.' Your reassuring tone of voice will help calm the dog as he tries to follow the food hand in order to get the treat.

When the dog's elbows touch the floor, release the food and praise softly. Try to get the dog to maintain that down position for several seconds before you let him sit up again. The goal here is to get the dog to settle down and not feel threatened in the down position.

Teaching Stay

It is easy to teach the dog to stay in either a sit or a down position. Again, we use food and praise during the teaching process as we help the dog to understand exactly what it is that we are expecting him to do.

To teach the sit/stay, start with the dog sitting on your left side as before and hold the lead in your left hand. Have a food treat in your right hand and place your food hand at the dog's nose. Say 'Stay' and step out on your right foot to stand directly in front of the dog, toe to toe, as he licks and nibbles the treat. Be sure to keep his head facing upward to maintain the sit position. Count to five and then swing around to stand next to the dog again with him on your left. As soon as you get back to the original position, release the food and praise lavishly.

To teach the down/stay, do the down as previously described. As soon as the dog lies down, say 'Stay' and step out on your right foot just as you did in the sit/stay. Count to five and then return to stand beside the dog with him on your left side. Release the treat and praise as always.

Within a week or ten days, you can begin to add a bit of distance between you and your dog when you leave him. When you do, use your left hand open with the palm facing the dog as a stay signal, much the same as the hand signal a constable uses to stop traffic at an intersection. Hold the food treat in your right hand as before, but this time the food is not touching the dog's nose. He will watch the food hand and quickly learn that he is going

Teach the stay with the dog in a sit position on your left side. Use hand signals to reinforce your commands.

to get that treat as soon as you return to his side.

When you can stand 1 metre away from your dog for 30 seconds, you can then begin building time and distance in both stays. Eventually, the dog can be expected to remain in the stay position for prolonged periods of time until you return to him or call him to you. Always praise lavishly when he stays.

TEACHING COME

If you make teaching 'Come' a positive experience, you should never have a 'student' that does not love the game or that fails to come when called. The secret, it seems, is never to teach the word 'Come.'

At times when an owner most wants his dog to come when called, the owner is likely upset or anxious and he allows these feelings to come through in the tone of his voice when he calls his dog. Hearing that desperation in his owner's voice, the dog fears the results of going to him and therefore either disobeys outright or runs in the opposite direction. The secret, therefore, is to teach the dog a game and, when you want him to come to you, simply play the game. It is practically a no-fail solution!

To begin, have several members of your family take a few food treats and each go into a different room in the house. Take turns calling the dog, and each person should celebrate the dog's finding him with a treat and lots of happy praise. When a person calls the dog, he is actually inviting the dog to find him and get a treat as a reward for 'winning.'

Arguably the most vital command you can teach your dog is heel. A well-behaved, happily heeling Clumber is a joy to walk for a few daily miles. This Clumber has not learned the heel command, and his owner is paying the price.

Heeling nicely by his owner's side, this Clumber is a daily pleasure for his master.

A few turns of the 'Where are you?' game and the dog will understand that everyone is playing the game and that each person has a big celebration awaiting his success at locating them. Once he learns to love the game, simply calling out 'Where are you?' will bring him running from wherever he is when he hears that all-important question.

The come command is recognised as one of the most important things to teach a dog, but there are trainers who work with thousands of dogs and never teach the actual word 'Come.' Yet these dogs will race to respond to a person who uses the dog's name followed by 'Where are you?' For example, a woman has a 12-year-old companion dog who went blind, but who never fails to locate her owner when asked, 'Where are you?'

Children particularly love to play this game with their dogs. Children can hide in smaller places like a shower or bath, behind a bed or under a table. The dog needs to work a little bit harder to find these hiding places, but when he does he loves to celebrate with a treat and a tussle with a favourite youngster.

Teaching Heel

Heeling means that the dog walks beside the owner without pulling. It takes time and patience on the owner's part to succeed at teaching the dog that he (the owner) will not proceed unless the dog is walking calmly beside him. Pulling out ahead on the lead is definitely not acceptable.

Begin with holding the lead in your left hand as the dog sits beside your left leg. Move the loop end of the lead to your right hand but keep your left hand short on the lead so it keeps the dog in close next to you.

Say 'Heel' and step forward on your left foot. Keep the dog close to you and take three steps. Stop and have the dog sit next to you in what we now call the 'heel position.' Praise verbally, but do not touch the dog. Hesitate a moment and begin again with 'Heel,' taking three steps and stopping, at which point the dog is told to sit again.

Your goal here is to have the dog walk those three steps without pulling on the lead. When he will walk calmly beside you for three steps without pulling, increase the number of steps you take to five. When he will walk politely beside you whilst you take five steps, you can increase the length of your walk to ten steps. Keep increasing the length of your stroll until the dog will walk quietly beside you without pulling as long as you want him to heel. When you stop heeling, indicate to the dog that the exercise is over by verbally praising as you pet him and say 'OK, good dog.' The 'OK' is used as a release word meaning that the exercise is finished and the dog is

TRAINING TIP

If you begin teaching the heel by taking long walks and letting the dog pull you along, he misinterprets this

action as an acceptable form of taking a walk. When you pull back on the lead to counteract his pulling, he reads that tug as a signal to pull even harder!

TRAINING TIP

Teach your dog to HEEL in an enclosed area. Once you think the dog will obey reliably and you want to attempt advanced obedience exercises such as off-lead heeling, test him in a fenced-in area so he cannot run away.

free to relax.

If you are dealing with a dog who insists on pulling you around, simply 'put on your brakes' and stand your ground until the dog realises that the two of you are not going anywhere until he is beside you and moving at your pace, not his. It may take some time just standing there to convince the dog that you are the leader and you will be the one to decide on the direction and speed of your travel.

Each time the dog looks up at you or slows down to give a slack lead between the two of you, quietly praise him and say, 'Good heel. Good dog.' Eventually, the dog will begin to respond and within a few days he will be walking politely beside you without pulling on the lead. At first, the training sessions should be kept short and very positive; soon the dog will be able to walk nicely with you for increasingly longer distances. Remember also to give the dog free time and the opportunity to run and play when you have finished heel practice.

WEANING OFF FOOD IN TRAINING

Food is used in training new behaviours. Once the dog understands what behaviour goes with a specific command, it is time to start weaning him off the food treats. At first, give a treat after each exercise. Then, start to give a treat only after every other exercise. Mix up the times when you offer a food reward and the times when you only offer praise so that the dog will never know

The stay command should be practised from the sit as well as the stand position. Be firm with your Clumber, but never harsh or unkind.

Most Clumbers have a favourite toy, which can be used to call the dog or to invite him to play.

when he is going to receive both food and praise and when he is going to receive only praise. This is called a variable ratio reward system and it proves successful because there is always the chance that the owner will produce a treat, so the dog never stops trying for that reward. No matter what, ALWAYS give verbal praise.

OBEDIENCE CLASSES

It is a good idea to enrol in an obedience class if one is available in your area. If yours is a show dog, ringcraft classes would be more appropriate. Many areas have dog clubs that offer basic obedience training as well as preparatory classes for obedience competition. There are also local dog trainers who offer similar classes.

At obedience trials, dogs can earn titles at various levels of competition. The beginning levels of competition include basic behaviours such as sit, down, heel, etc. The more advanced levels of competition include jumping, retrieving, scent discrimination and signal work. The advanced levels require a dog and owner to put a lot of time and effort into their training and the titles that can be earned at these levels of competition are very prestigious.

OTHER ACTIVITIES FOR LIFE

Whether a dog is trained in the structured environment of a class or alone with his owner at home, there are many activities that can bring fun and rewards to both owner and dog once they have mastered basic control.

Teaching the dog to help out around the home, in the garden or on the farm, provides great satisfaction to both dog and owner. In addition, the dog's help makes life a little easier for his owner and raises his stature as a valued companion to his family. It helps give the dog a purpose by

TRAINING TIP

A dog in jeopardy never lies down. He stays alert on his feet because instinct tells him that he may have to run away or fight for his survival. Therefore, if a dog feels threatened or anxious, he will not lie down. Consequently, it is important to have the dog calm and relaxed as he learns the down exercise.

Who says that Clumbers are lazy?! Engage your Clumber in a vigorous game of fetch and he will come to life and play like a puppy.

occupying his mind and providing an outlet for his energy.

Hiking is an exciting and healthy activity that the dog can be taught without assistance from more than his owner. The exercise of walking and climbing is good for man and dog alike, and the bond that they develop together is priceless.

If you are interested in participating in organised competition with your Clumber Spaniel, there are activities other than obedience in which you and your dog can become involved. Agility is a popular sport where dogs run through an obstacle course that includes various jumps, tunnels and other exercises to test the dog's speed and coordination. The owners run through the course beside their dogs to give commands and to guide them through the course. Although competitive, the focus is on fun—it's fun to do, fun to watch, and great exercise.

Physical Structure of the Clumber Spaniel

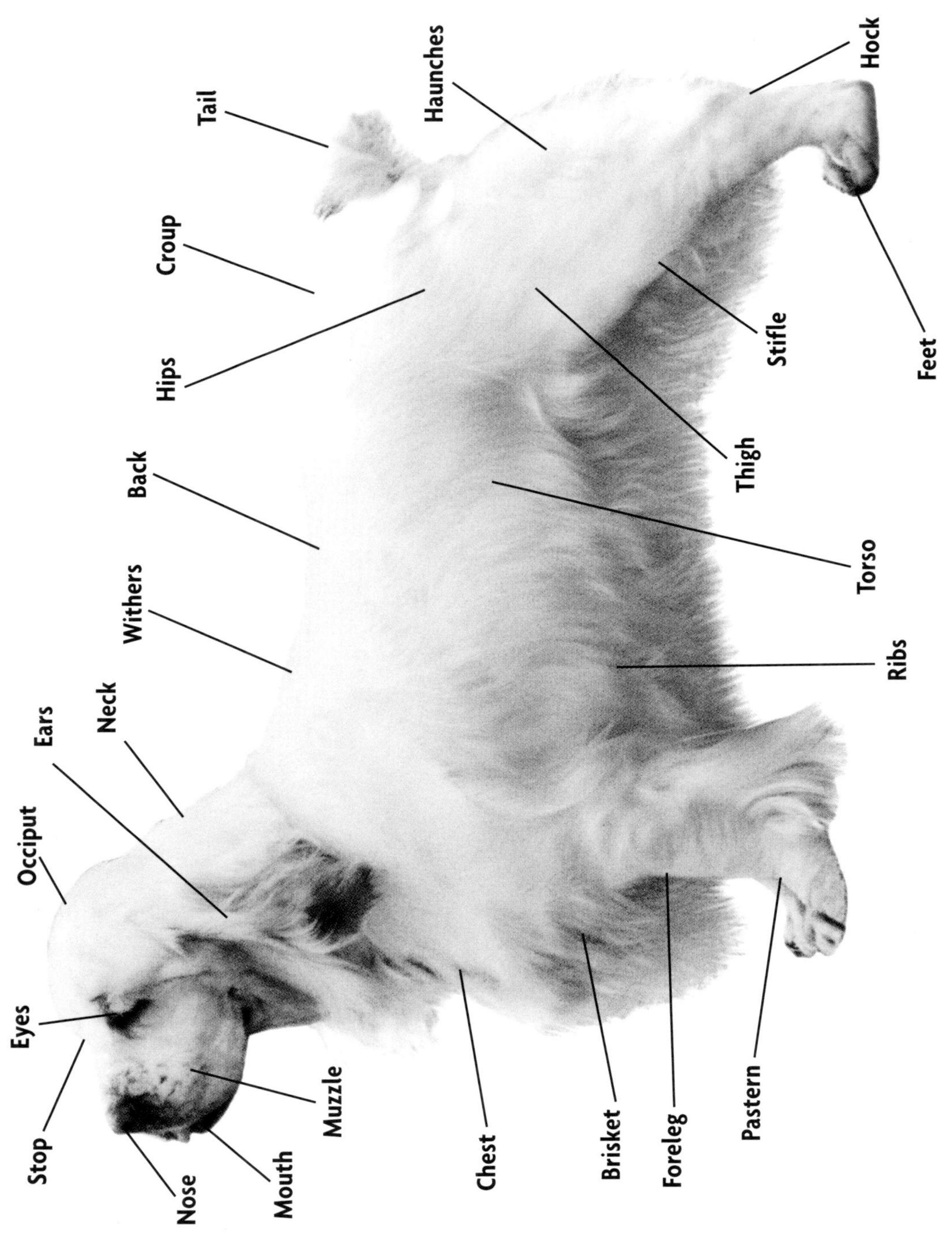

HEALTH CARE OF YOUR
CLUMBER SPANIEL

Dogs suffer many of the same physical illnesses as people. They might even share many of the same psychological problems. Since people usually know more about human diseases than canine maladies, many of the terms used in this chapter will be familiar but not necessarily those used by veterinary surgeons. We will use the term *x-ray*, instead of the more acceptable term *radiograph*. We will also use the familiar term *symptoms* even though dogs don't have symptoms, which are verbal descriptions of the patient's feelings: dogs have *clinical signs*. Since dogs can't speak, we have to look for clinical signs...but we still use the term *symptoms* in this book.

As a general rule, medicine is *practised*. That term is not arbitrary. Medicine is a constantly changing art as we learn more and more about genetics, electronic aids (like CAT scans) and daily laboratory advances. There are many dog maladies, like entropion and canine hip dysplasia, which are not universally treated in the same manner. Some veterinary surgeons opt for surgery more often than others do.

SELECTING A VETERINARY SURGEON

Your selection of a veterinary surgeon should not be based upon personality (as most are) but upon his convenience to your home. You want a veterinary surgeon who is close because you might have emergencies or need to make multiple visits for treatments. You want a vet who has services that you might require such as tattooing and grooming facilities, as well as sophisticated pet supplies and a good reputation for ability and responsiveness. There

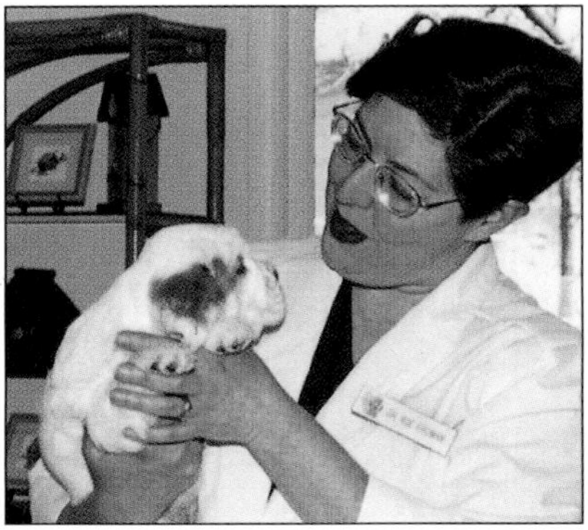

Dr Roe Froman is a veterinary surgeon who specialises in Clumber Spaniels. Here she is shown examining a four-week-old Clumber puppy to evaluate its general health.

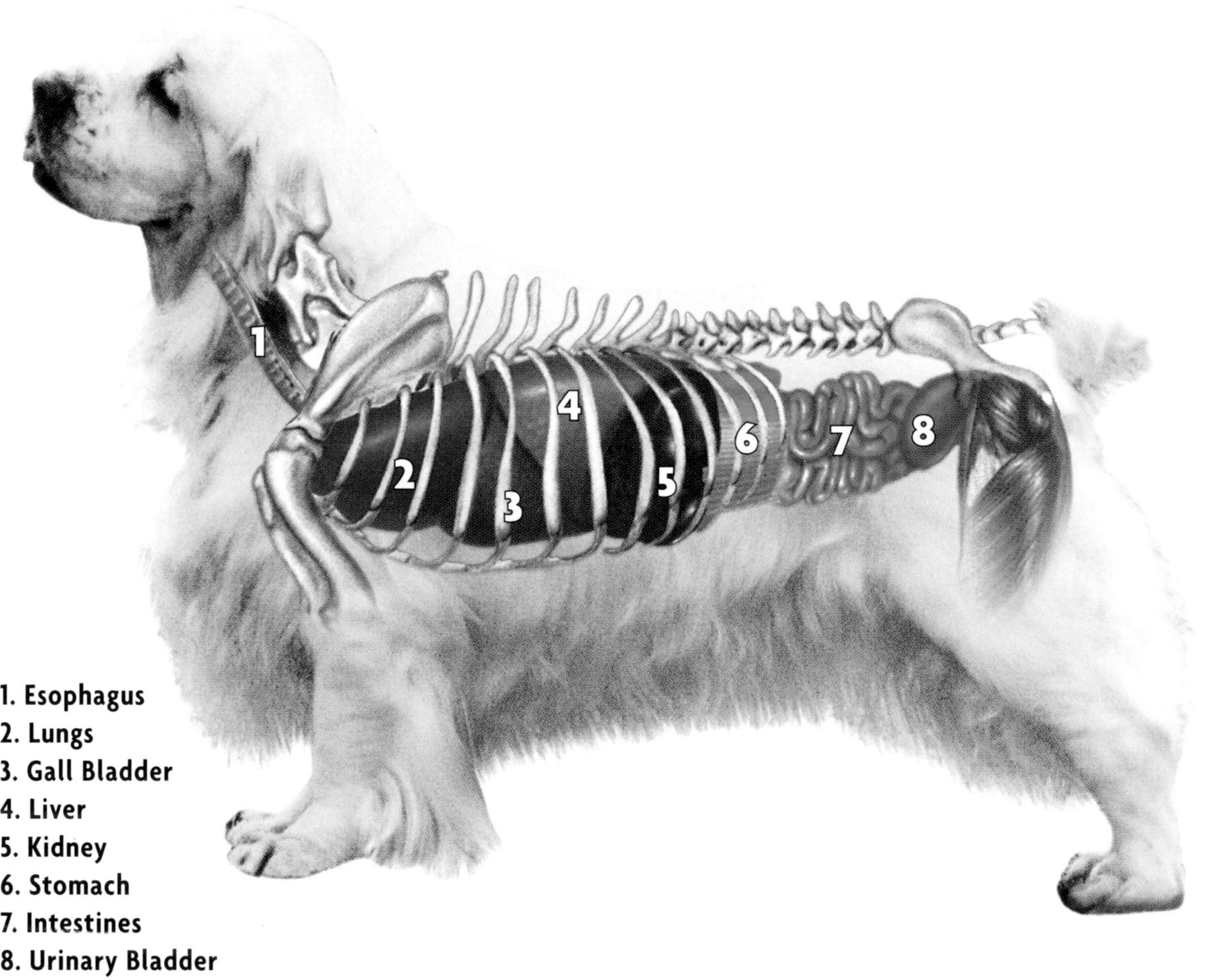

Internal Organs of the Clumber Spaniel

is nothing more frustrating than having to wait a day or more to get a response from your veterinary surgeon.

All veterinary surgeons are licensed and their diplomas and/or certificates should be displayed in their waiting rooms. There are, however, many veterinary specialities that usually require further studies and internships. There are specialists in heart problems (veterinary cardiologists), skin problems (veterinary dermatologists), teeth and gum problems (veterinary dentists), eye problems (veterinary ophthalmologists), x-rays (veterinary radiologists), and surgeons who have specialities in bones, muscles or other organs. Most veterinary surgeons do routine surgery such as neutering, stitching up wounds and docking tails for those breeds in which such is required for show purposes. When the problem affecting your dog is serious, it is not unusual or impudent to get another medical opinion, although in Britain you are obliged to advise the vets concerned about this. You might also want to compare costs amongst several veterinary surgeons. Sophisticated health care and veterinary services can be very costly. Don't be bashful about discussing these costs with your veterinary surgeon or his staff. It is not infrequent that important decisions are based upon financial considerations.

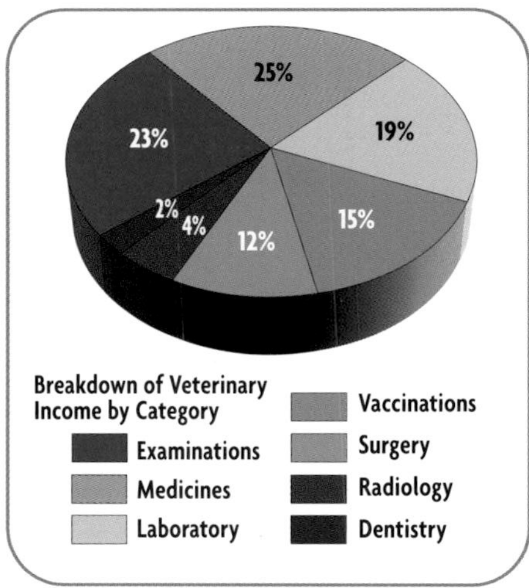

A typical American vet's income, categorised according to services provided. This survey dealt with small-animal practices.

DID YOU KNOW?

Male dogs are neutered. The operation removes the testicles and requires that the dog be anaesthetised. Recovery takes about one week. Females are spayed. This is major surgery and it usually takes a bitch two weeks to recover.

PREVENTATIVE MEDICINE

It is much easier, less costly and more effective to practise preventative medicine than to fight bouts of illness and disease. Properly bred puppies come from parents that were selected based upon their genetic disease profile. Their mothers should have been vaccinated, free of all internal and external parasites, and properly

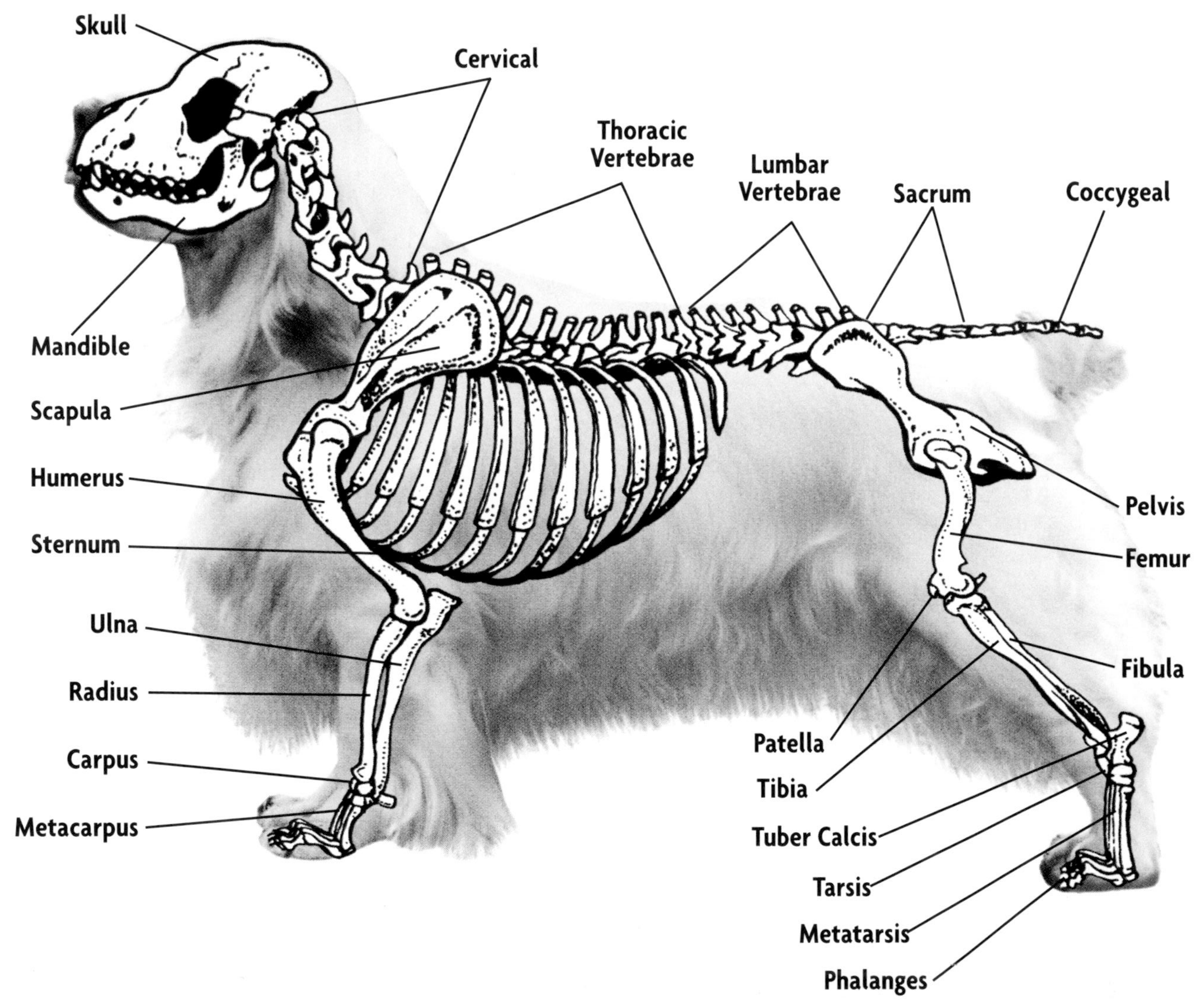

Skeletal Structure of the Clumber Spaniel

nourished. For these reasons, a visit to the veterinary surgeon who cared for the dam (mother) is recommended. The dam can pass on disease resistance to her puppies, which can last for eight to ten weeks. She can also pass on parasites and many infections. That's why you should visit the veterinary surgeon who cared for the dam.

Weaning to Five Months Old

Puppies should be weaned by the time they are about two months old. A puppy that remains for at least eight weeks with its mother and littermates usually adapts better to other dogs and people later in its life.

Some new owners have their puppy examined by a veterinary surgeon immediately, which is a good idea. Vaccination programmes usually begin when the puppy is very young.

DID YOU KNOW?

Dogs who have been exposed to lawns sprayed with herbicides have double and triple the rate of malignant lymphoma. Town dogs are especially at risk, as they are exposed to tailored lawns and gardens. Dogs perspire and absorb through their footpads. Be careful where your dog walks and always avoid any area that appears yellowed from chemical overspray.

Once the puppy has reached the age of three or four months, he should undergo a veterinary examination to check for potential problems of the eyes, skin and back. Discuss this with your vet and breeder.

The puppy will have its teeth examined and have its skeletal conformation and general health checked prior to certification by the veterinary surgeon. Puppies in certain breeds have problems with their kneecaps, eye cataracts and other eye problems, heart murmurs and undescended testicles. If possible, try to find a vet with Clumber experience. The shape of the Clumber's eyelids is different, with a diamond-shaped lower lid. This sometimes leads to mistaken recommendations for surgical corrections, which may not be needed. Since the Clumber Spaniel is a relatively uncommon breed, vets who are familiar with them are often happy to consult with the breeder's veterinary surgeon.

HEALTH AND VACCINATION SCHEDULE

AGE IN WEEKS:	6TH	8TH	10TH	12TH	14TH	16TH	20-24TH	1 YR
Worm Control	✔	✔	✔	✔	✔	✔	✔	
Neutering								✔
Heartworm*		✔		✔		✔	✔	
Parvovirus	✔		✔		✔		✔	✔
Distemper		✔		✔		✔		✔
Hepatitis		✔		✔		✔		✔
Leptospirosis								✔
Parainfluenza	✔		✔		✔			✔
Dental Examination		✔					✔	✔
Complete Physical		✔					✔	✔
Coronavirus				✔			✔	✔
Kennel Cough	✔							
Hip Dysplasia								✔
Rabies*							✔	

Vaccinations are not instantly effective. It takes about two weeks for the dog's immunization system to develop antibodies. Most vaccinations require annual booster shots. Your veterinary surgeon should guide you in this regard.

*Not applicable in the United Kingdom

Puppies may also have personality problems and your veterinary surgeon might have training in temperament evaluation.

VACCINATION SCHEDULING

Most vaccinations are given by injection and should only be done by a veterinary surgeon. Both he and you should keep a record of the date of the injection, the identification of the vaccine and the amount given. Some vets give a first vaccination at eight weeks, but most dog breeders prefer the course not to commence until about ten weeks because of negating any antibodies passed on by the dam. The vaccination scheduling is usually based on a 15-day cycle. You must take your vet's advice as to when to vaccinate as this may differ according to the vaccine used. Most vaccinations immunize your puppy against viruses.

The usual vaccines contain immunizing doses of several different viruses, such as distemper, parvovirus, parainfluenza and hepatitis. There are other vaccines available when the puppy is at risk. You should rely upon professional advice. This is especially true for the booster-shot programme. Most vaccination programmes require a booster when the puppy is a year old and once a year thereafter. In some cases, circumstances may require more or less frequent immunizations.

Kennel cough, more formally known as tracheobronchitis, is treated with a vaccine that is sprayed into the dog's nostrils. Kennel cough is usually included in routine vaccination, but this is often not so effective as for other major diseases.

DID YOU KNOW?

Vaccines do not work all the time. Sometimes dogs are allergic to them and many times the antibodies, which are supposed to be stimulated by the vaccine, just are not produced. You should keep your dog in the veterinary clinic for an hour after it is vaccinated to be sure there are no allergic reactions.

Five Months to One Year of Age

During his physical examination, your dog should be evaluated for

DISEASE REFERENCE CHART

	What is it?	What causes it?	Symptoms
Leptospirosis	Severe disease that affects the internal organs; can be spread to people.	A bacterium, which is often carried by rodents, that enters through mucous membranes and spreads quickly throughout the body.	Range from fever, vomiting and loss of appetite in less severe cases to shock, irreversible kidney damage and possibly death in most severe cases.
Rabies	Potentially deadly virus that infects warm-blooded mammals. Not seen in United Kingdom.	Bite from a carrier of the virus, mainly wild animals.	1st stage: dog exhibits change in behaviour, fear. 2nd stage: dog's behaviour becomes more aggressive. 3rd stage: loss of coordination, trouble with bodily functions.
Parvovirus	Highly contagious virus, potentially deadly.	Ingestion of the virus, which is usually spread through the faeces of infected dogs.	Most common: severe diarrhoea. Also vomiting, fatigue, lack of appetite.
Kennel cough	Contagious respiratory infection.	Combination of types of bacteria and virus. Most common: *Bordetella bronchiseptica* bacteria and parainfluenza virus.	Chronic cough.
Distemper	Disease primarily affecting respiratory and nervous system.	Virus that is related to the human measles virus.	Mild symptoms such as fever, lack of appetite and mucous secretion progress to evidence of brain damage, 'hard pad.'
Hepatitis	Virus primarily affecting the liver.	Canine adenovirus type I (CAV-1). Enters system when dog breathes in particles.	Lesser symptoms include listlessness, diarrhoea, vomiting. More severe symptoms include 'blue-eye' (clumps of virus in eye).
Coronavirus	Virus resulting in digestive problems.	Virus is spread through infected dog's faeces.	Stomach upset evidenced by lack of appetite, vomiting, diarrhoea.

DID YOU KNOW?

A dental examination is in order when the dog is between six months and one year of age so any permanent teeth that have erupted incorrectly can be corrected. It is important to begin a brushing routine, preferably using a two-sided brushing technique, whereby both sides of the tooth are brushed at the same time. Durable nylon and safe edible chews should be a part of your puppy's arsenal for good health, good teeth and pleasant breath. The vast majority of dogs three to four years old and older has diseases of the gums from lack of dental attention. Using the various types of dental chews can be very effective in controlling dental plaque.

the common hip dysplasia plus other diseases of the joints. There are tests to assist in the prediction of these problems. Other tests can also be run, such as the parvovirus antibody titer, which can assess the effectiveness of the vaccination programme.

Unless you intend to breed or show your dog, neutering the puppy at six months of age is recommended. Discuss this with your veterinary surgeon.

By the time your Clumber Spaniel is seven or eight months of age, he can be seriously evaluated for his conformation to the breed standard, thus determining show potential and desirability as a sire or dam. If the puppy is not top class and therefore is not a candidate for a serious breeding programme, most professionals advise neutering the puppy. Neutering has proven to be extremely beneficial to both male and female puppies. Besides the obvious impossibility of pregnancy, it inhibits breast cancer in bitches and prostate problems in male dogs. Under no circumstances should a bitch be spayed prior to her first season.

Eosinophilic panosteitis, often known as pano or eolan, is a condition similar to 'growing pains.' It is frequently seen in adolescent pups between seven and fifteen months of age. It manifests as an intermittent, shifting leg lameness. That is, the dog will be lame on different legs at different times. Diagnosis of this condition by your veterinary surgeon is relatively straightforward, based on physical examination, clinical signs and sometimes x-rays (although typical lesions consistent with this diagnosis often are most noticeable in unaffected legs, making x-ray interpretation a bit more difficult). Although panosteitis can cause puppies to be quite lame, they typically feel fine otherwise, and eating and drinking habits remain normal. Mild pain-killing or anti-inflammatory medicines may bring some comfort, but the true cure for this condition is tincture of time (time itself).

A blood test can be performed for heartworm infestation and it is possible that your puppy will be placed on a preventative therapy that will prevent heartworm infection as well as control other internal parasites.

Your veterinary surgeon should provide your puppy with a thorough dental evaluation at six months of age, ascertaining whether all the permanent teeth have erupted properly. A home dental care regimen should be initiated at six months, including brushing weekly and providing good dental devices (such as nylon bones). Regular dental care promotes healthy teeth, fresh breath and a longer life.

One to Seven Years

Once a year, your grown dog should visit the vet for an examination and vaccination boosters. Some vets recommend blood tests, thyroid level check and dental evaluation to accompany these annual visits. A thorough clinical evaluation by the vet can provide critical background information for your dog. Blood tests are often performed at one year of age, and dental examinations around the third or fourth birthday. In the long run, quality preventative care for your pet can save money, teeth and lives.

INTERVERTEBRAL DISC DISEASE

Long, low and heavy set, Clumber Spaniels are anatomically, if not genetically as well, predisposed to disc disease. In this condition, the cushioning disc between adjacent vertebrae in the spine ruptures or herniates. This puts pressure on the spinal cord, leading to back pain, lameness, reluctance to turn or move the neck, and sometimes, paralysis. Two areas may be affected on Clumbers: the cervical region (neck), or the thoracolumbar area (back). Episodes often manifest as acute onset of pain (reluctance to move, inability to get up, reluctance to turn head or neck, lameness) with periods of remission between flare-ups.

Diagnosis is based upon clinical signs, physical examination, x-rays or myelography (the injection of dye into the spinal canal to identify the exact location of the problem). Treatment is either medical or surgical, depending on location. Cervical discs can respond very well to surgery performed by a practitioner qualified in the procedure. Thoracolumbar disc surgery is most often performed by neurosurgeons. Medical

Frolicking about is a most natural behaviour for dogs. Sound vertebral health is essential to dogs being able to act like dogs.

therapy consisting of corticosteroids and strict crate rest for three weeks are often very helpful.

SKIN PROBLEMS IN CLUMBER SPANIELS

Veterinary surgeons are consulted by dog owners for skin problems more than any other group of diseases or maladies. Dogs' skin is almost as sensitive as human skin and both suffer almost the same ailments. (Though the occurrence of acne in dogs is rare!) For this reason, veterinary dermatology has developed into a speciality practised by many veterinary surgeons.

Since many skin problems have visual symptoms that are almost identical, it requires the skill of an experienced veterinary dermatologist to identify and cure many of the more severe skin disorders. Pet shops sell many treatments for skin problems but most of the treatments are directed at symptoms and not the underlying problem(s). If your dog is suffering from a skin disorder, you should seek professional assistance as quickly as possible. As with all diseases, the earlier a problem is identified and treated, the more successful is the cure.

Hereditary Skin Disorders

Veterinary dermatologists are currently researching a number of skin disorders that are believed to have a hereditary basis. These inherited diseases are transmitted by both parents, who appear (phenotypically) normal but have a recessive gene for the disease, meaning that they carry, but are not affected by, the disease. These diseases pose serious problems to breeders because in some instances there is no method of identifying carriers. Often the secondary diseases associated with these skin conditions are even more debilitating than the skin disorder, including cancers and respiratory problems; others can be lethal.

Amongst the hereditary skin disorders, for which the mode of inheritance is known, are acrodermatitis, cutaneous asthenia (Ehlers-Danlos syndrome), sebaceous adenitis, cyclic hematopoiesis, dermatomyositis, IgA deficiency, colour dilution alopecia and nodular dermatofibrosis. Some of these disorders are limited to one or

A SKUNKY PROBLEM

Have you noticed your dog dragging his rump along the floor? If so, it is likely that his anal sacs are impacted or possibly infected. The anal sacs are small pouches located on both sides of the anus under the skin and muscles. They are about the size and shape of a grape and contain a foul-smelling liquid. Their contents are usually emptied when the dog has a bowel movement, but if they are not emptied completely, they will impact, which will cause your dog a lot of pain. Fortunately, your veterinary surgeon can tend to this problem easily by draining the sacs for the dog. Be aware that your dog might also empty his anal sacs in cases of extreme fright.

Along with the sunshine and soft green grass, the summer months usher in the flea season. Closely examine your Clumber's coat after he's been lying about the garden.

two breeds and others affect a large number of breeds. All inherited diseases must be diagnosed and treated by a veterinary specialist.

Parasite Bites

Many of us are allergic to insect bites. The bites itch, erupt and may even become infected. Dogs have the same reaction to fleas, ticks and/or mites. When an insect lands on you, you have the chance to whisk it away with your hand. Unfortunately, when your dog is bitten by a flea, tick or mite, it can only scratch it away

DID YOU KNOW?

By the time your dog is a year old, you should have become very comfortable with your veterinary surgeon and have agreed on scheduling visits for booster vaccinations. Blood tests should be taken regularly for comparative purposes, for such variables as cholesterol and triglyceride levels, thyroid hormones, liver enzymes, blood cell counts, etc. The yearly exam should also include a thorough teeth cleaning.

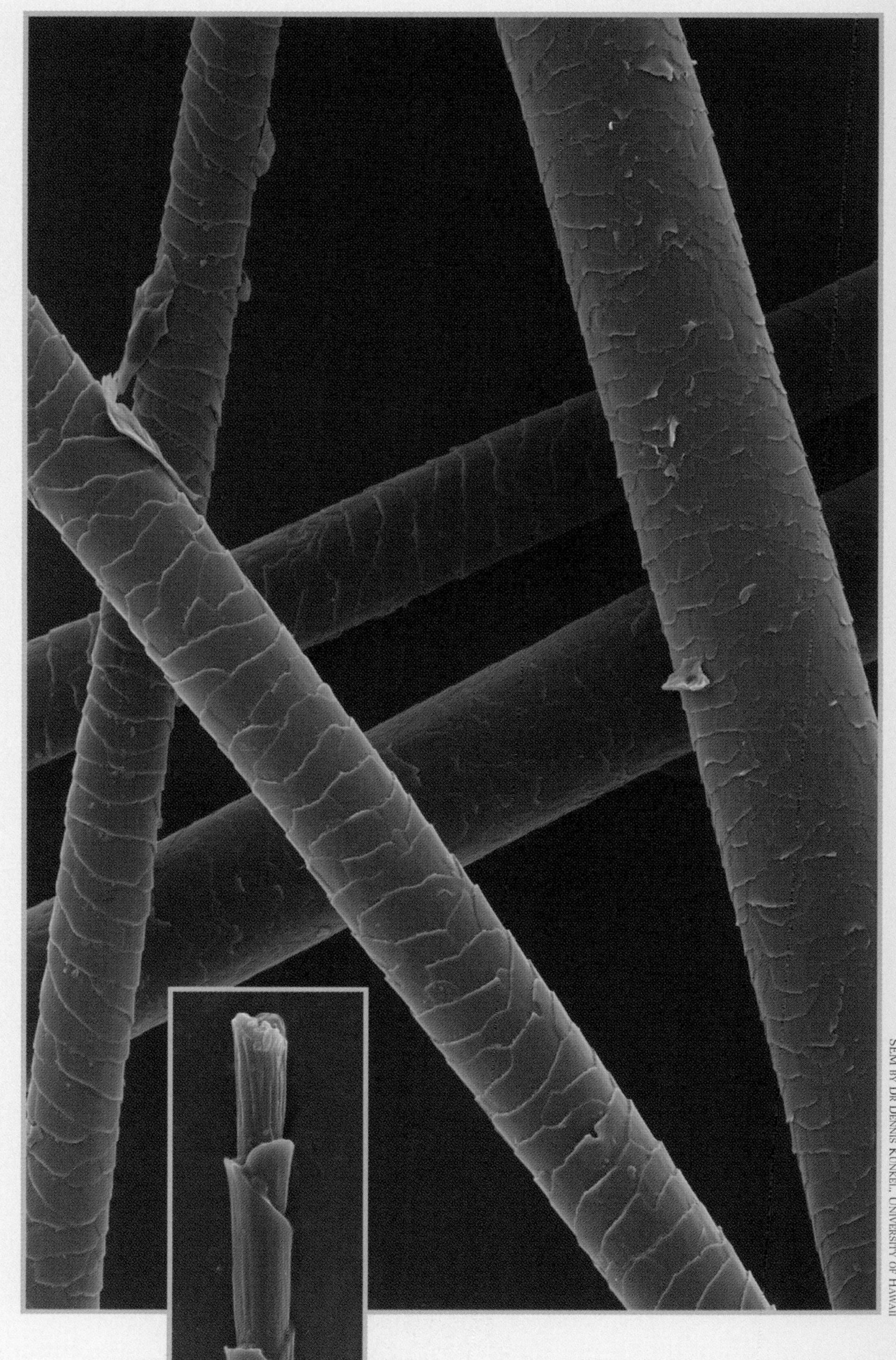

Normal hairs of a dog enlarged 200 times original size. The cuticle (outer covering) is clean and healthy. Unlike human hair that grows from the base, dog's hair also grows from the end, as shown in the inset. Scanning electron micrographs by Dr Dennis Kunkel, University of Hawaii.

SEM by Dr Dennis Kunkel, University of Hawaii

or bite it. By the time the dog has been bitten, the parasite has done some of its damage. It may also have laid eggs to cause further problems in the near future. The itching from parasite bites is probably due to the saliva injected into the site when the parasite sucks the dog's blood.

Airborne Allergies

An interesting allergy is pollen allergy. Humans have hay fever, rose fever and other fevers with which they suffer during the pollinating season. Many dogs suffer the same allergies. When the pollen count is high, your dog might suffer but don't expect him to sneeze and have a runny nose like humans. Dogs react to pollen allergies the same way they react to fleas—they scratch and bite themselves.

Dogs, like humans, can be tested for allergens. Discuss the testing with your veterinary dermatologist.

FOOD PROBLEMS

Food Allergies

Dogs are allergic to many foods that are best-sellers and highly recommended by breeders and veterinary surgeons. Changing the brand of food that you buy may not eliminate the problem if the element to which the dog is allergic is contained in the new brand.

Food allergies can be exasperating to solve. Once a food allergy has been positively identified, an owner must make a complete commitment to changing and controlling the dog's diet.

Recognising a food allergy is difficult. Humans vomit or have rashes when they eat a food to which they are allergic. Dogs neither vomit nor (usually) develop a rash. They react in the same manner as they do to an airborne or flea allergy: they itch, scratch and bite. Thus making the

DID YOU KNOW?

The myth that dogs need extra fat in their diets can be harmful. Should your vet recommend extra fat, use safflower oil instead of animal oils. Safflower oil has been shown to be less likely to cause allergic reactions.

Don't Eat the Daisies!

Many plants and flowers are beautiful to look at, but can be highly toxic if ingested by your dog. Reactions range from abdominal pain and vomiting to convulsions and death. If the following plants are in your home, remove them. If they are outside your house or in your garden, avoid accidents by making sure your dog is never left unsupervised in those locations.

- Azalea
- Belladonna
- Bird of Paradise
- Bulbs
- Calla lily
- Cardinal flower
- Castor bean
- Chinaberry tree
- Daphne
- Dumb cane
- Dutchman's breeches
- Elephant's ear
- Hydrangea
- Jack-in-the-pulpit
- Jasmine
- Jimsonweed
- Larkspur
- Laurel
- Lily of the valley
- Mescal bean
- Mushrooms
- Nightshade
- Philodendron
- Poinsettia
- Prunus species
- Tobacco
- Yellow jasmine
- Yews, Taxus species

diagnosis extremely difficult. Whilst pollen allergies and parasite bites are usually seasonal, food allergies are year-round problems.

Food Intolerance

Food intolerance is the inability of the dog to completely digest certain foods. Puppies that may have done very well on their mother's milk may not do well on cow's milk. The result of this food intolerance may be loose bowels, passing gas and stomach pains. These are the only obvious symptoms of food intolerance and that makes diagnosis difficult.

Treating Food Problems

It is possible to handle food allergies and food intolerance yourself. Put your dog on a diet that it has never had. Obviously if it has never eaten this new food it can't have been allergic or intolerant of it. Start with a single ingredient that is not in the dog's diet at the present time. Ingredients like chopped beef or fish are common in dogs' diets, so try something more exotic like rabbit, pheasant or even just vegetables. Keep the dog on this diet (with no additives) for a month. If the symptoms of food allergy or intolerance disappear, chances are

DID YOU KNOW?

Cases of hyperactive adrenal glands (Cushing's disease) have been traced to the drinking of highly chlorinated water. Aerate or age your dog's drinking water before offering it.

your dog has a food allergy.

Don't think that the single ingredient cured the problem. You still must find a suitable diet and ascertain which ingredient in the old diet was objectionable. This is most easily done by adding ingredients to the new diet one at a time. Let the dog stay on the modified diet for a month before you add another ingredient. Eventually, you will determine the ingredient that caused the adverse reaction.

An alternative method is to carefully study the ingredients in the diet to which your dog is allergic or intolerant. Identify the main ingredient in this diet and eliminate it by buying a different food that does not have that ingredient. Keep experimenting until the symptoms disappear after one month on the new diet.

Your Clumber relies upon you in times of sickness and health. Owning a Clumber is a long-time commitment.

Handling food allergies and food intolerance is often accomplished via hypoallergenic diets. It is important for these diets to be nutritionally balanced. They are based on novel carbohydrates and protein sources (ingredients the dog has never eaten before). These may include venison, rabbit, duck and potato. While a dog is on a food trial, it is important to avoid incidental protein sources, such as treats or rawhides. Consult your veterinary surgeon who may also be able to provide you with a homecooked, completely balanced hypoallergenic diet.

DID YOU KNOW?

Chances are that you and your dog will have the same allergies. Your allergies are readily recognizable and usually easily treated. Your dog's allergies may be masked.

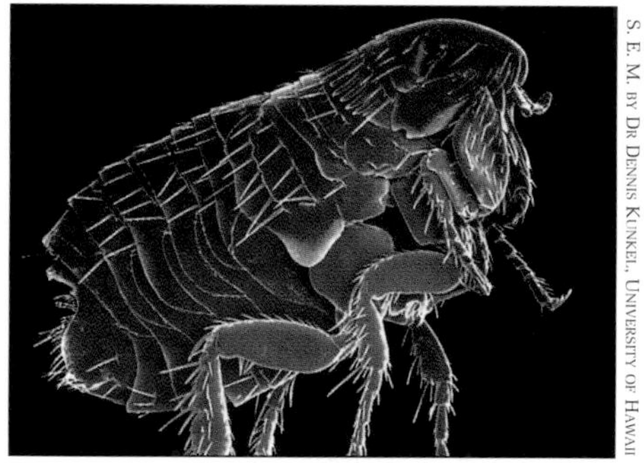

A scanning electron micrograph (S. E. M.) of a dog flea, *Ctenocephalides canis.*

S. E. M. by Dr Dennis Kunkel, University of Hawaii

EXTERNAL PARASITES

Of all the problems to which dogs are prone, none is more well known and frustrating than fleas. Flea infestation is relatively simple to cure but difficult to prevent. Parasites that are harboured inside the body are a bit more difficult to eradicate but they are easier to control.

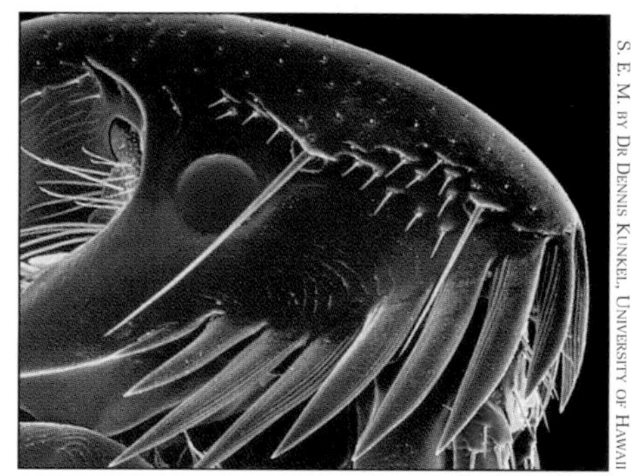

Magnified head of a dog flea, *Ctenocephalides canis.*

S. E. M. by Dr Dennis Kunkel, University of Hawaii

FLEAS

To control a flea infestation you have to understand the flea's life cycle. Fleas are often thought of as a summertime problem but centrally heated homes have changed the patterns and fleas can be found at any time of the year. The most effective method of flea control is a two-stage approach:

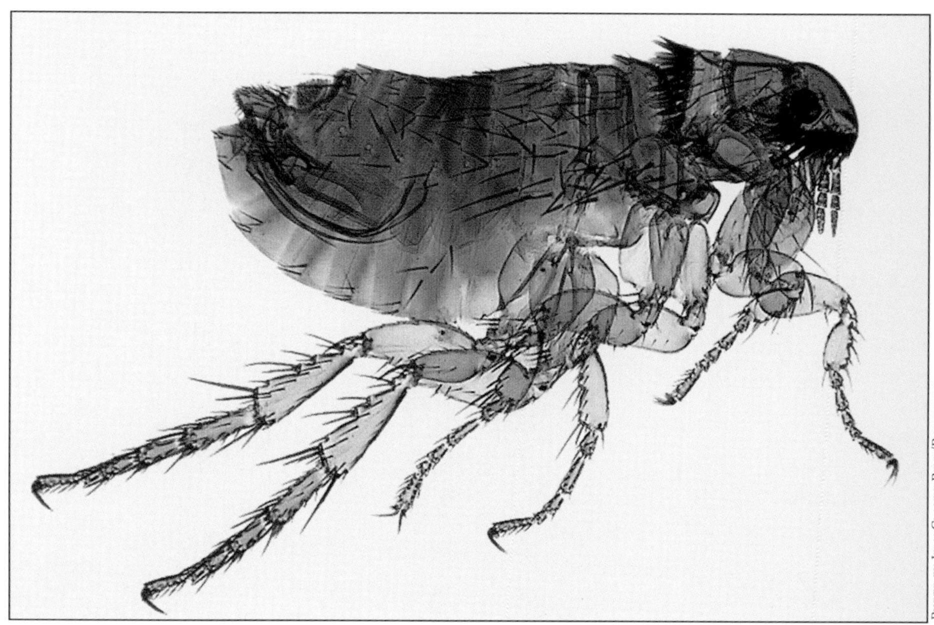

A male dog flea, *Ctenocephalides canis.*

Photo by Jean Claude Revy/Phototake.

DID YOU KNOW?

Flea-killers are poisonous. You should not spray these toxic chemicals on areas of a dog's body that he licks, on his genitals or on his face. Flea killers taken internally are a better answer, but check with your vet in case internal therapy is not advised for your dog.

one stage to kill the adult fleas, and the other to control the development of pre-adult fleas. Unfortunately, no single active ingredient is effective against all stages of the life cycle.

Life Cycle Stages

During its life, a flea will pass through four life stages: egg, larva, pupa and adult. The adult stage is the most visible and irritating stage of the flea life cycle and this is why the majority of flea-control products concentrate on this stage. The fact is that adult fleas account for only 1% of the total flea population, and the other 99% exist in pre-adult stages, i.e. eggs, larvae and pupae. The pre-adult stages are barely visible to the naked eye.

The Life Cycle of the Flea

Eggs are laid on the dog, usually in quantities of about 20 or 30, several times a day. The female adult flea must have a blood meal before each egg-laying session. When first laid, the eggs will cling to the dog's fur, as the eggs are still moist. However, they will quickly dry out and fall from the dog, especially if the dog moves around or scratches. Many eggs will fall off in the dog's favourite area or an area in which he spends a lot of time, such as his bed.

Once the eggs fall from the dog onto the carpet or furniture, they will hatch into larvae. This takes from one to ten days. Larvae are not particularly mobile, and will usually travel only a few inches from where they hatch. However, they do have a tendency to move

A Look at Fleas

Fleas have been around for millions of years and have adapted to changing host animals. They are able to go through a complete life cycle in less than one month or they can extend their lives to almost two years by remaining as pupae or cocoons. They do not need blood or any other food for up to 20 months.

They have been measured as being able to jump 300,000 times and can jump 150 times their length in any direction including straight up. Those are just a few of the reasons why they are so successful in infesting a dog!

Illustration Courtesy of Bayer Vital GmbH & Co. KG

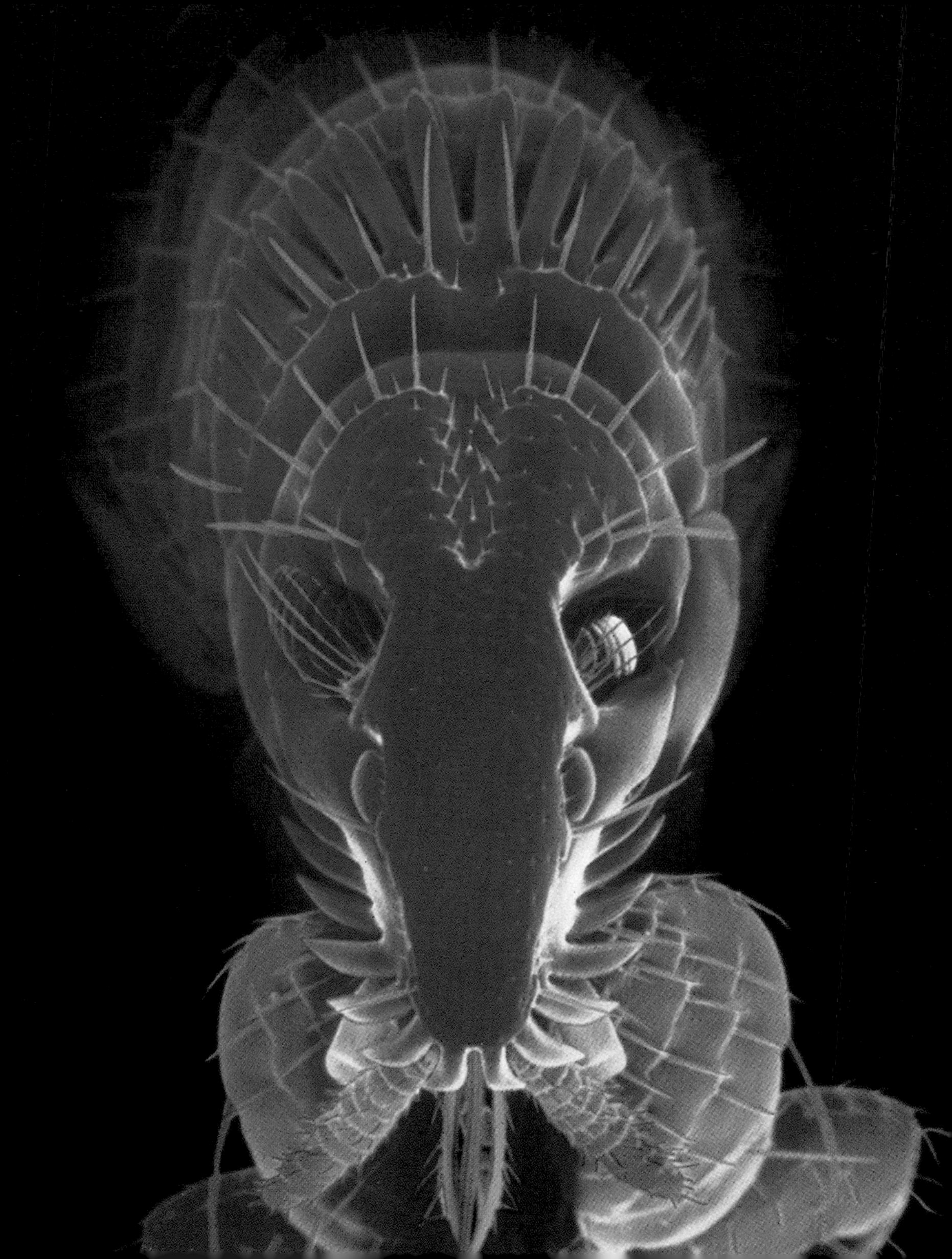

away from light and heavy traffic—under furniture and behind doors are common places to find high quantities of flea larvae.

The flea larvae feed on dead organic matter, including adult flea faeces, until they are ready to change into adult fleas. Fleas will usually remain as larvae for around seven days. After this period, the larvae will pupate into protective pupae. While inside the pupae, the larvae will undergo metamorphosis and change into adult fleas. This can take as little time as a few days, but the adult fleas can remain inside the pupae waiting to hatch for up to two years. The pupae are signalled to hatch by certain stimuli, such as physical pressure—the pupae's being stepped on, heat from an animal lying on the pupae or increased carbon dioxide levels and vibrations—indicating that a suitable host is available.

Once hatched, the adult flea must feed within a few days. Once the adult flea finds a host, it will not leave voluntarily. It only becomes dislodged by grooming or the host animal's scratching. The adult flea will remain on the host for the duration of its life unless forcibly removed.

En Garde: CATCHING FLEAS OFF GUARD

Consider the following ways to arm yourself against fleas:

- Add a small amount of pennyroyal or eucalyptus oil to your dog's bath. These natural remedies repel fleas.
- Supplement your dog's food with fresh garlic (minced or grated) and a hearty amount of brewer's yeast, both of which ward off fleas.
- Use a flea comb on your dog daily. Submerge fleas in a cup of bleach to kill them quickly.
- Confine the dog to only a few rooms to limit the spread of fleas in the home.
- Vacuum daily...and get all of the crevices! Dispose of the bag every few days until the problem is under control.
- Wash your dog's bedding daily. Cover cushions where your dog sleeps with towels, and wash the towels often.

DID YOU KNOW?

Never mix flea control products without first consulting your veterinary surgeon. Some products can become toxic when combined with others and can cause serious or fatal consequences.

TREATING THE ENVIRONMENT AND THE DOG

Treating fleas should be a two-pronged attack. First, the environment needs to be treated; this includes carpets and furniture, especially the dog's bedding and

Opposite page: A scanning electron micrograph of a dog or cat flea, *Ctenocephalides*, magnified more than 100x. This image has been colourized for effect.

The Life Cycle of the Flea

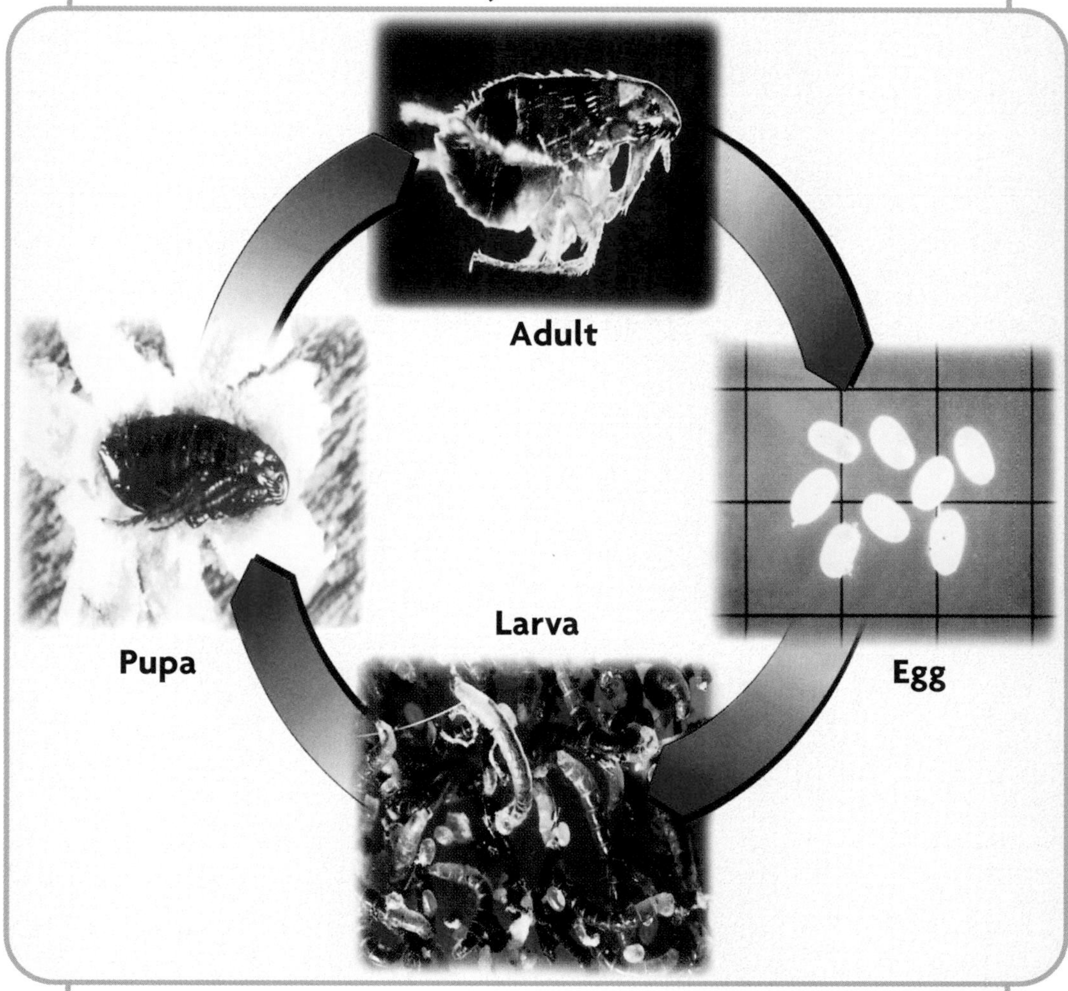

This graphic depiction of the life cycle of the flea appears courtesy of Fleabusters®, R_x for fleas.

areas underneath furniture. The environment should be treated with a household spray containing an Insect Growth Regulator (IGR) and an insecticide to kill the adult fleas. Most IGRs are effective against eggs and larvae; they actually mimic the fleas' own hormones and stop the eggs and larvae from developing into adult fleas. There are currently no treatments available to attack the pupa stage of the life cycle, so the adult insecticide is used to kill the newly hatched adult fleas before

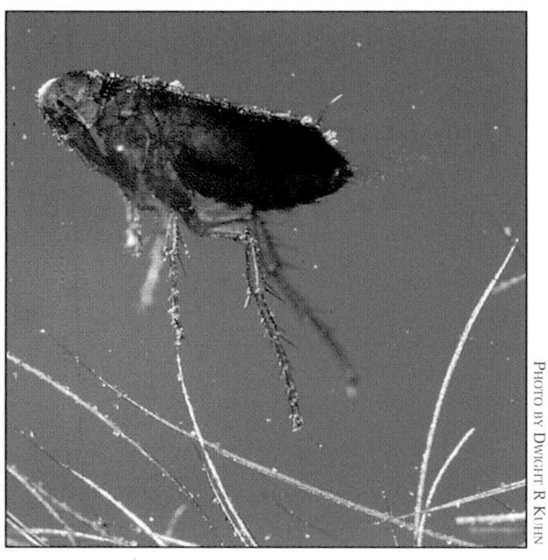

PHOTO BY DWIGHT R KUHN

Dwight R Kuhn's magnificent action photo showing a flea jumping from a dog's back.

they find a host. Most IGRs are active for many months, whilst adult insecticides are only active for a few days.

When treating with a household spray, it is a good idea to vacuum before applying the product. This stimulates as many pupae as possible to hatch into adult fleas. The vacuum cleaner should also be treated with a flea treatment to prevent the eggs and larvae that have been hoovered into the vacuum bag from hatching.

The second stage of treatment is to apply an adult insecticide to the dog. Traditionally, this would be in the form of a collar or a spray, but more recent innovations include digestible insecticides that poison the fleas when they ingest the dog's blood. Alternatively, there are drops that, when placed on the back of the animal's neck, spread throughout the fur and skin to kill adult fleas.

Ticks and Mites

Though not as common as fleas, ticks and mites are found all over the tropical and temperate world. They don't bite, like fleas; they harpoon. They dig their sharp proboscis (nose) into the dog's skin and drink the blood. Their only food and drink is dog's blood. Dogs can get Lyme disease, Rocky Mountain spotted fever (normally

FLEA CONTROL

Two types of products should be used when treating fleas—a product to treat the pet and a product to treat the home. Adult fleas represent less than 1% of the flea population. The pre-adult fleas (eggs, larvae and pupae) represent more than 99% of the flea population and are found in the environment; it is in the case of pre-adult fleas that products containing an Insect Growth Regulator (IGR) should be used in the home.

IGRs are a new class of compounds used to prevent the development of insects. They do not kill the insect outright, but instead use the insect's biology against it to stop it from completing its growth. Products that contain methoprene are the world's first and leading IGRs. Used to control fleas and other insects, this type of IGR will stop flea larvae from developing and protect the house for up to seven months.

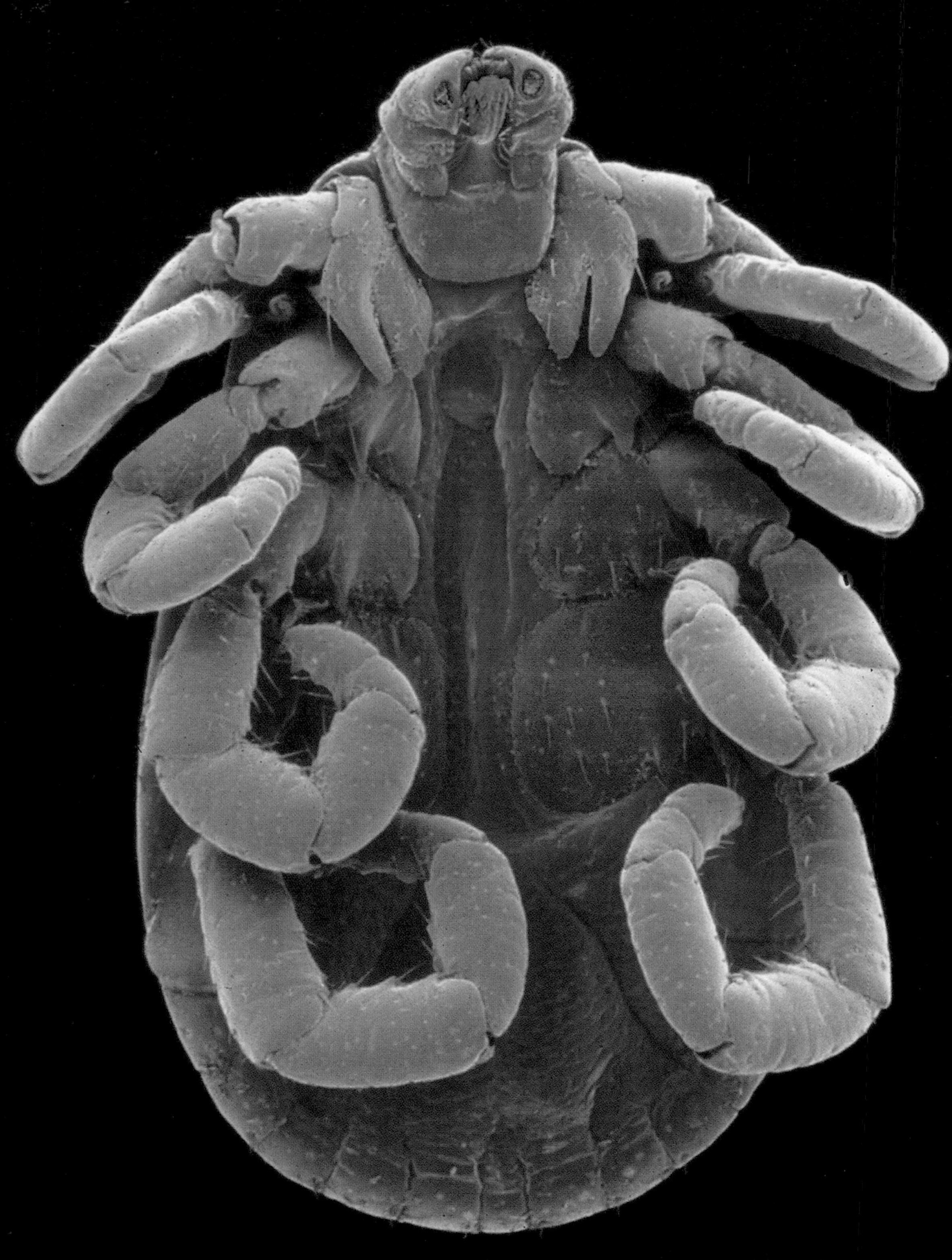

found in the US only), paralysis and many other diseases from ticks and mites. They may live where fleas are found and they like to hide in cracks or seams in walls wherever dogs live. They are controlled the same way fleas are controlled.

The dog tick, *Dermacentor variabilis*, may well be the most common dog tick in many geographical areas, especially those areas where the climate is hot and humid.

Most dog ticks have life expectancies of a week to six

ILLUSTRATION COURTESY OF BAYER VITAL GMBH & CO. KG

Beware the Deer Tick

The great outdoors may be fun for your dog, but it also is a home to dangerous ticks. Deer ticks carry a bacterium known as *Borrelia burgdorferi* and are most active in the autumn and spring. When infections are caught early, penicillin and tetracycline are effective antibiotics, but if left untreated the bacteria may cause neurological, kidney and cardiac problems as well as long-term trouble with walking and painful joints.

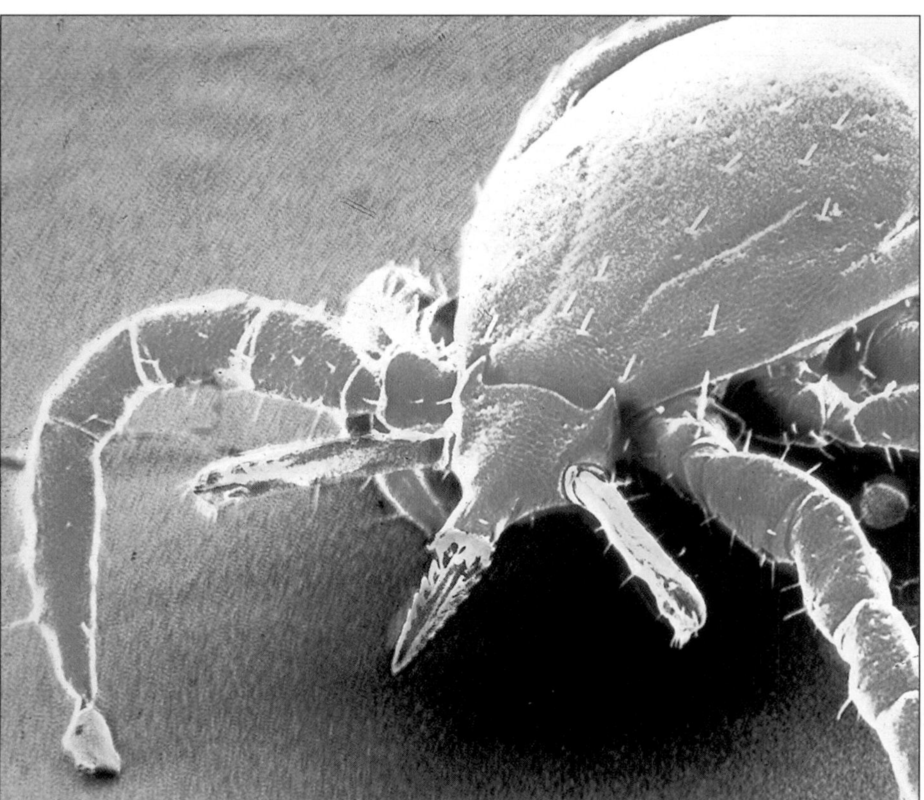

S. E. M. BY DR ANDREW SPIELMAN/PHOTOTAKE

A deer tick, the carrier of Lyme disease. This magnified micrograph has been colourized for effect.

Opposite page: The dog tick, *Dermacentor variabilis*, is probably the most common tick found on dogs. Look at the strength in its eight legs! No wonder it's hard to detach them.

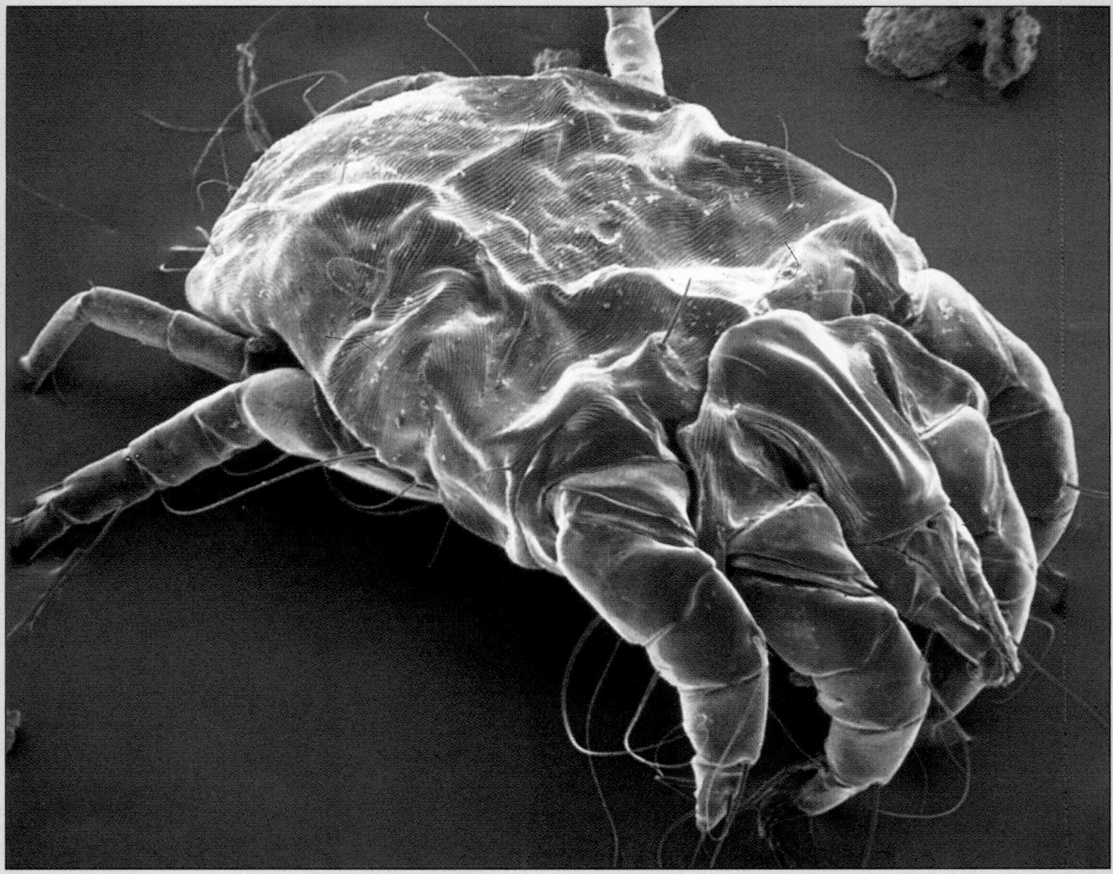

Photo by James Hayden-Yoav/Phototake.

Above:
The mange mite,
Psoroptes bovis.

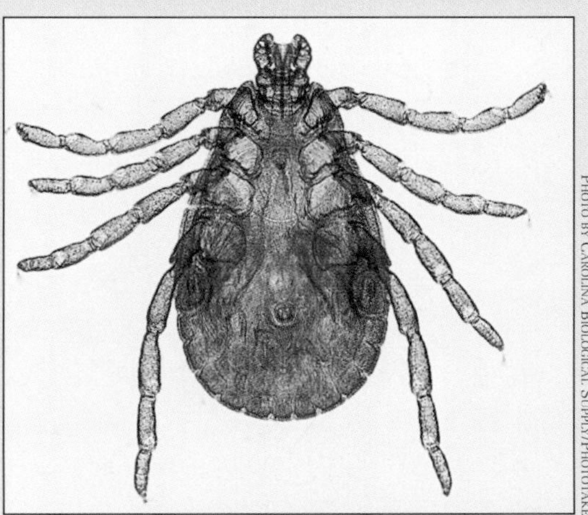

Photo by Carolina Biological Supply/Phototake

A brown dog tick, *Rhipicephalus sanguineus*, is an uncommon but annoying tick found on dogs.

Photo by Dwight R Kuhn

Human lice look like dog lice; the two are closely related

months, depending upon climatic conditions. They can neither jump nor fly, but they can crawl slowly and can range up to 5 metres (16 feet) to reach a sleeping or unsuspecting dog.

Mange

Mites cause a skin irritation called mange. Some are contagious, like *Cheyletiella*, ear mites, scabies and chiggers. Mites that cause ear-mite infestations are usually controlled with Lindane, which can only be administered by a vet, followed by Tresaderm at home.

It is essential that your dog be treated for mange as quickly as possible because some forms of mange are transmissible to people.

INTERNAL PARASITES

Most animals—fishes, birds and mammals, including dogs and humans—have worms and other parasites that live inside their bodies. According to Dr Herbert R Axelrod, the fish pathologist, there are two kinds of parasites: dumb and smart. The smart parasites live in peaceful cooperation with their hosts (symbiosis), while the dumb parasites kill their host. Most of the worm infections are relatively easy to control. If they are not controlled they weaken the host dog to the point that other medical problems occur, but they are not dumb parasites.

Roundworms

The roundworms that infect dogs are scientifically known as *Toxocara canis*. They live in the dog's intestine. The worms shed eggs continually. It has been estimated that a dog produces about 150 grammes of faeces every day. Each gramme of faeces averages 10,000–12,000 eggs of roundworms. There are no known areas in which dogs roam that do not contain roundworm eggs. The greatest danger of roundworms is that they infect people too! It is

DEWORMING

Ridding your puppy of worms is VERY IMPORTANT because certain worms that puppies carry, such as tapeworms and roundworms, can infect humans.

Breeders initiate a deworming programme at or about four weeks of age. The routine is repeated every two or three weeks until the puppy is three months old. The breeder from whom you obtained your puppy should provide you with the complete details of the deworming programme.

Your veterinary surgeon can prescribe and monitor the programme of deworming for you. The usual programme is treating the puppy every 15–20 days until the puppy is positively worm free.

It is not advised that you treat your puppy with drugs that are not recommended professionally.

wise to have your dog tested regularly for roundworms.

Pigs also have roundworm infections that can be passed to humans and dogs. The typical roundworm parasite is called *Ascaris lumbricoides.*

HOOKWORMS

The worm *Ancylostoma caninum* is commonly called the dog hookworm. It is dangerous to humans and cats. It also has teeth by which it attaches itself to the intestines of the dog. It changes the site of its attachment about six times a day and the dog loses blood from each detachment, possibly causing iron-deficiency anaemia. Hookworms are easily purged from the dog with many medications. Milbemycin oxime,

ROUNDWORMS

Average size dogs can pass 1,360,000 roundworm eggs every day.

For example, if there were only 1 million dogs in the world, the world would be saturated with 1,300 metric tonnes of dog faeces.

These faeces would contain 15,000,000,000 roundworm eggs.

It's known that 7–31% of home gardens and children's play boxes in the US contain roundworm eggs.

Flushing dog's faeces down the toilet is not a safe practice because the usual sewage treatments do not destroy roundworm eggs.

Infected puppies start shedding roundworm eggs at 3 weeks of age. They can be infected by their mother's milk.

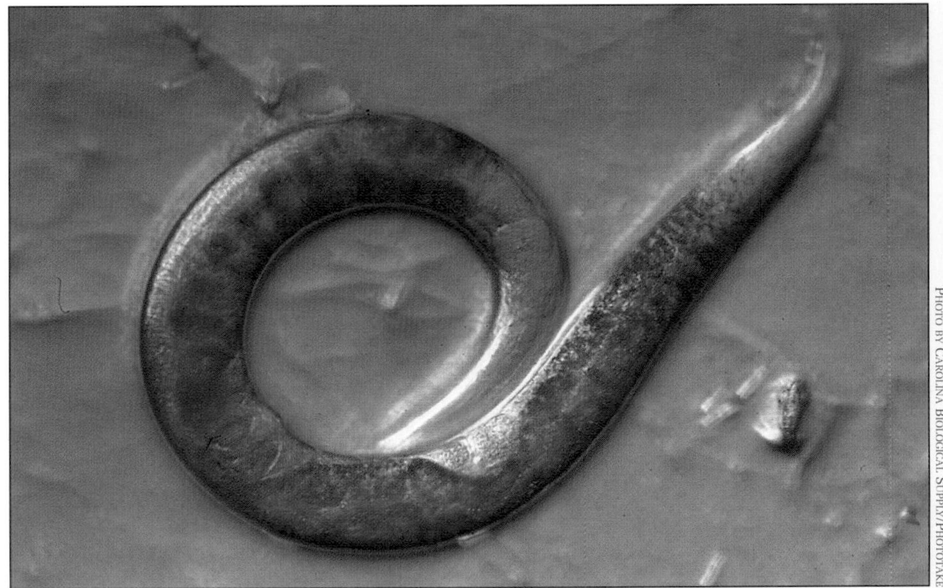

The roundworm, *Rhabditis*. The roundworm can infect both dogs and humans.

PHOTO BY CAROLINA BIOLOGICAL SUPPLY/PHOTOTAKE

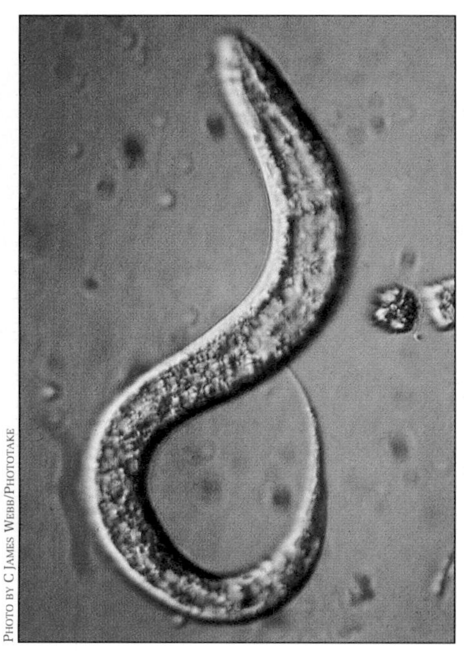

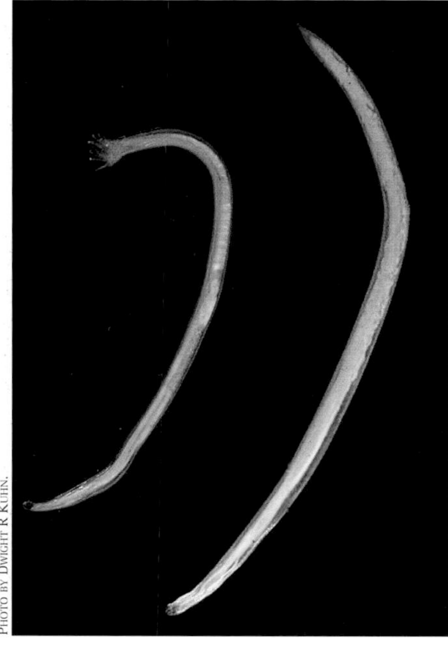

Left:
The infective stage of the hookworm larva.

Right:
Male and female hookworms, *Ancylostoma caninum*, are uncommonly found in pet or show dogs in Britain. Hookworms may infect other dogs that have exposure to grasslands.

which also serves as a heartworm preventative in Collies, can be used for this purpose.

In Britain the 'temperate climate' hookworm (*Uncinaria stenocephala*) is rarely found in pet or show dogs, but can occur in hunting packs, racing Greyhounds and sheepdogs because the worms can be prevalent wherever dogs are exercised regularly on grassland.

DID YOU KNOW?

Never allow your dog to swim in polluted water or public areas where water quality can be suspect. Even perfectly clear water can harbour parasites, many of which can cause serious to fatal illnesses in canines. Areas inhabited by waterfowl and other wildlife are especially dangerous.

TAPEWORMS

There are many species of tapeworms. They are carried by fleas! The dog eats the flea and starts the tapeworm cycle. Humans can also be infected with tapeworms, so don't eat fleas! Fleas are so small that your dog could pass them onto your hands, your plate or your food and thus make it possible for you to ingest a flea which is carrying tapeworm eggs.

While tapeworm infection is not life threatening in dogs (smart parasite!), it can be the cause of a

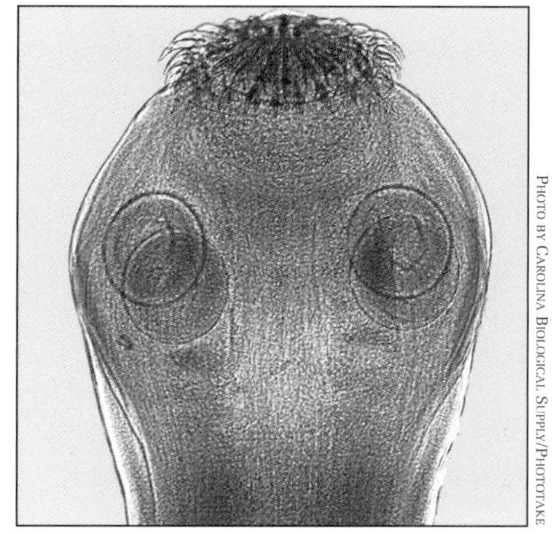
PHOTO BY CAROLINA BIOLOGICAL SUPPLY/PHOTOTAKE

The head and rostellum (the round prominence on the scolex) of a tapeworm, which infects dogs and humans.

very serious liver disease for humans. About 50 percent of the humans infected with *Echinococcus multilocularis*, a type of tapeworm that causes alveolar hydatis, perish.

TAPEWORMS

Humans, rats, squirrels, foxes, coyotes, wolves, mixed breeds of dogs and purebred dogs are all susceptible to tapeworm infection. Except in humans, tapeworms are usually not a fatal infection.

Infected individuals can harbour a thousand parasitic worms.

Tapeworms have two sexes—male and female (many other worms have only one sex—male and female in the same worm).

If dogs eat infected rats or mice, they get the tapeworm disease.

One month after attaching to a dog's intestine, the worm starts shedding eggs. These eggs are infective immediately.

Infective eggs can live for a few months without a host animal.

Roundworms, whipworms and hookworms are just a few of the other commonly known worms that infect dogs.

HEARTWORMS

Heartworms are thin, extended worms up to 30 cms (12 ins) long which live in a dog's heart and the major blood vessels surrounding it. Dogs may have up to 200 worms. Symptoms may be loss of energy, loss of appetite, coughing, the development of a pot belly and anaemia.

Heartworms are transmitted by mosquitoes. The mosquito drinks the blood of an infected dog and takes in larvae with the blood. The larvae, called microfilaria, develop within the body of the mosquito and are passed on to the next dog bitten after the larvae mature. It takes two to three weeks for the larvae to develop to the infective stage within the body of the mosquito. Dogs should be treated at about six weeks of age, and maintained on a prophylactic dose given monthly.

Blood testing for heartworms is not necessarily indicative of how seriously your dog is infected. This is a dangerous disease. Although heartworm is a problem for dogs in America, Australia, Asia and Central Europe, dogs in the United Kingdom are not currently affected by heartworm.

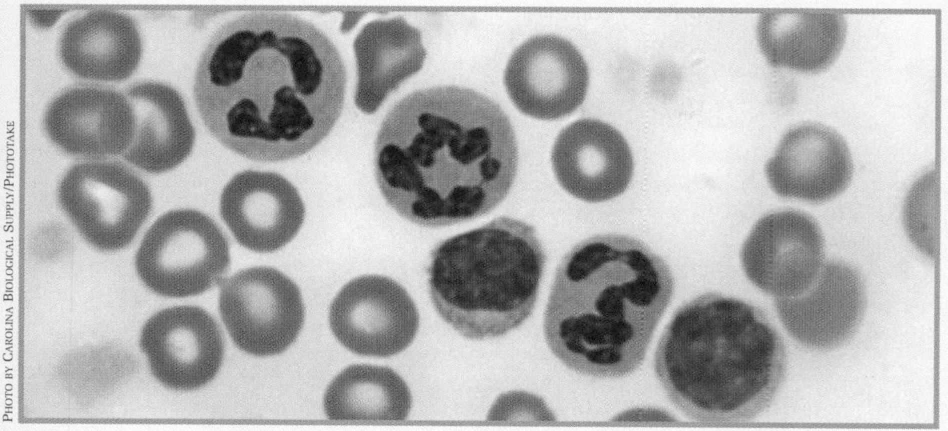

Photo by Carolina Biological Supply/Phototake

Magnified heartworm larvae, *Dirofilaria immitis.*

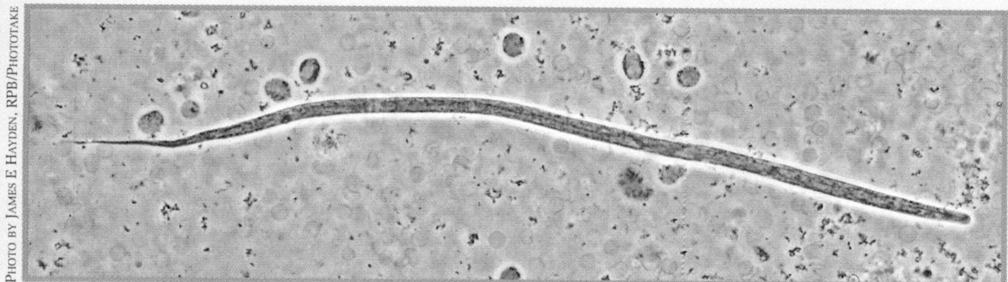

Photo by James E Hayden, RPB/Phototake

The heartworm, *Dirofilaria immitis.*

Photo by James E Hayden, RPB/Phototake

The heart of a dog infected with canine heartworm, *Dirofilaria immitis.*

Vitamins Recommended for Dogs

Some breeders and vets recommend the supplementation of vitamins to a dog's diet—others do not. Before embarking on a vitamin programme, consult your vet.

Vitamin / Dosage	Food source	Benefits
A / 10,000 IU/week	Eggs, butter, yoghurt, meat	Skin, eyes, hind legs, haircoat
B / Varies	Organs, cottage cheese, sardines	Appetite, fleas, heart, skin and coat
C / 2000 mg+	Fruit, legumes, leafy green vegetables	Healing, arthritis, kidneys
D / Varies	Cod liver, cheese, organs, eggs	Bones, teeth, endocrine system
E / 250 IU daily	Leafy green vegetables, meat, wheat germ oil	Skin, muscles, nerves, healing, digestion
F / Varies	Fish oils, raw meat	Heart, skin, coat, fleas
K / Varies	Naturally in body, not through food	Blood clotting

PET ADVANTAGES

If you do not intend to show or breed your new puppy, your veterinary surgeon will probably recommend that you spay your female or neuter your male. Some people believe neutering leads to weight gain, but if you feed and exercise your dog properly, this is easily avoided. Spaying or neutering can actually have many positive outcomes, such as:

- training becomes easier, as the dog focuses less on the urge to mate and more on you!
- females are protected from unplanned pregnancy as well as ovarian and uterine cancers.
- males are guarded from testicular tumours and have a reduced risk of developing prostate cancer.

Talk to your vet regarding the right age to spay/neuter and other aspects of the procedure.

First Aid at a Glance

Burns
Place the affected area under cool water; use ice if only a small area is burnt.

Bee/Insect bites
Apply ice to relieve swelling; antihistamine dosed properly.

Animal bites
Clean any bleeding area; apply pressure until bleeding subsides; go to the vet.

Spider bites
Use cold compress and a pressurised pack to inhibit venom's spreading.

Antifreeze poisoning
Induce vomiting with hydrogen peroxide. Seek *immediate* veterinary help!

Fish hooks
Removal best handled by vet; hook must be cut in order to remove.

Snake bites
Pack ice around bite; contact vet quickly; identify snake for proper antivenin.

Car accident
Move dog from roadway with blanket; seek veterinary aid.

Shock
Calm the dog, keep him warm; seek immediate veterinary help.

Nosebleed
Apply cold compress to the nose; apply pressure to any visible abrasion.

Bleeding
Apply pressure above the area; treat wound by applying a cotton pack.

Heat stroke
Submerge dog in cold bath; cool down with fresh air and water; go to the vet.

Frostbite/Hypothermia
Warm the dog with a warm bath, electric blankets or hot water bottles.

Abrasions
Clean the wound and wash out thoroughly with fresh water; apply antiseptic.

Remember: an injured dog may attempt to bite a helping hand from fear and confusion. Always muzzle the dog before trying to offer assistance.

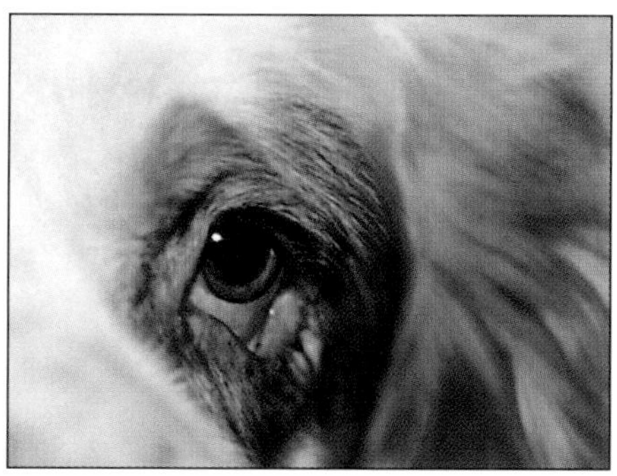

This is an example of a good eye on a Clumber Spaniel. The eyelids do not turn in nor out; the diamond-shaped lower lid is typical for the breed.

A PET OWNER'S GUIDE TO COMMON OPHTHALMIC DISEASES

by Prof. Dr Robert L Peiffer, Jr.

Few would argue that vision is the most important of the cognitive senses, and maintenance of a normal visual system is important for an optimal quality of life. Likewise, pet owners tend to be acutely aware of their pet's eyes and vision, which is important because early detection of ocular disease will optimize therapeutic outcomes. The eye is a sensitive organ with minimal reparative capabilities, and with some diseases, such as glaucoma, uveitis and retinal detachment, delay in diagnosis and treatment can be critical in terms of whether vision can be preserved.

The causes of ocular disease are quite varied; the nature of dogs make them susceptible to traumatic conditions, the most common of which include proptosis of the globe, cat scratch injuries and penetrating wounds from foreign objects, including sticks and air rifle pellets. Infectious diseases caused by bacteria, viruses or fungi may be localized to the eye or part of a systemic infection. Many of the common conditions, including eyelid conformational problems, cataracts, glaucoma and retinal degenerations have a genetic basis.

Before acquiring your puppy it is important to ascertain that both parents have been examined and certified free of eye disease by a veterinary ophthalmologist. Since many of these genetic diseases can be detected early in life, acquire the pup with the condition that it pass a thorough ophthalmic examination by a qualified specialist.

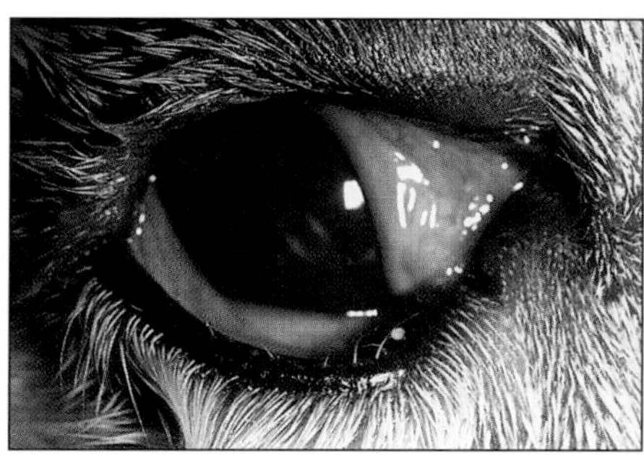

Lower entropion, or rolling in of the eyelid, is causing irritation in the left eye of this young dog. Several extra eyelashes, or distichiasis, are present on the upper lid.

Lid Conformational Abnormalities

Rolling in (entropion) or out (ectropion) of the lids tends to be a breed-related problem. Entropion can involve the upper and/or lower lids. Signs usually appear between 3 and 12 months of age. The irritation caused by the eyelid hairs rubbing

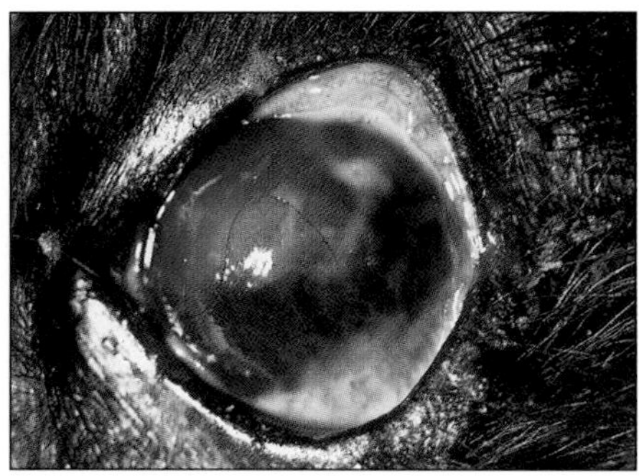

Keratoconjunctivitis sicca, seen here in the right eye of a middle-aged dog, causes a characteristic thick mucous discharge as well as secondary corneal changes.

on the surface of the cornea may result in blinking, tearing and damage to the cornea. Ectropion is likewise breed-related and is considered 'normal' in hounds, for instance; unlike entropion, which results in acute discomfort, ectropion may cause chronic irritation related to exposure and the pooling of secretions. Most of these cases can be managed medically with daily irrigation with sterile saline and topical antibiotics when required.

Eyelash Abnormalities

Dogs normally have lashes only on the upper lids, in contrast to humans. Occasionally, extra eyelashes may be seen emerging at the eyelid margin (distichiasis) or through the inner surface of the eyelid (ectopic cilia).

Conjunctivitis

Inflammation of the conjunctiva, the pink tissue that lines the lids and the anterior portion of the sclera, is generally accompanied by redness, discharge and mild discomfort. The majority of cases are either associated with bacterial infections or dry eye syndrome. Fortunately, topical medications are generally effective in curing or controlling the problem.

Dry Eye Syndrome

Dry eye syndrome (keratoconjunctivitis sicca) is a common cause of external ocular disease. Discharge is typically thick and sticky, and keratitis is a frequent component; any breed can be affected. While some cases can be associated with toxic effects of drugs, including the sulfa antibiotics, the cause in the majority of the cases cannot be determined and is assumed to be immune-mediated.

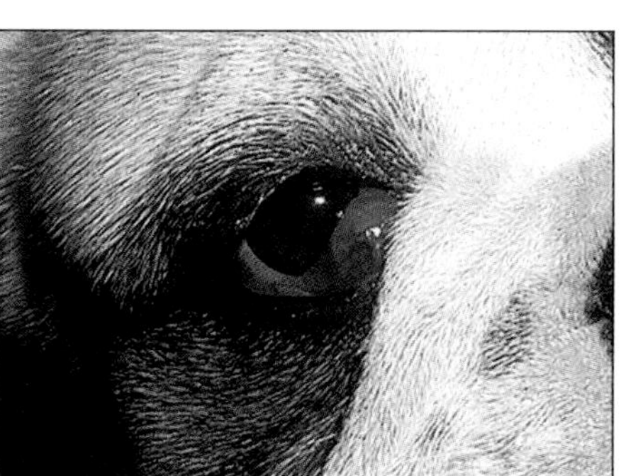

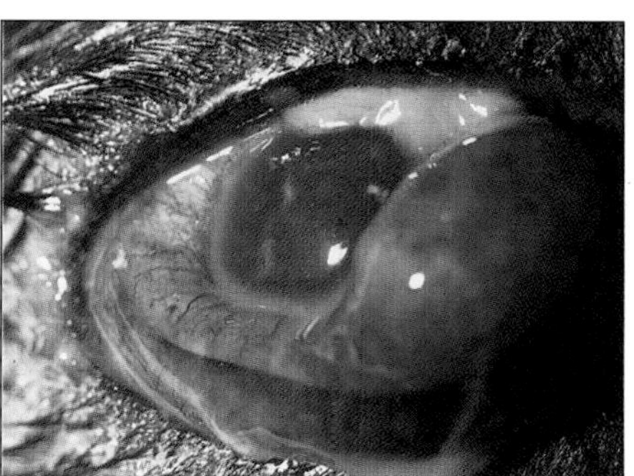

Left: Prolapse of the gland of the third eyelid in the right eye of a pup. Right: In this case, in the right eye of a young dog, the prolapsed gland can be seen emerging between the edge of the third eyelid and the corneal surface.

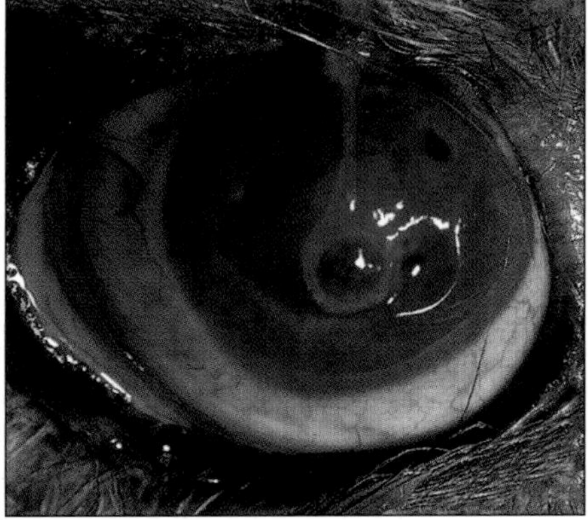

Multiple deep ulcerations affect the cornea of this middle-aged dog.

Prolapse of the Gland of the Third Eyelid

In this condition, commonly referred to as *cherry eye*, the gland of the third eyelid, which produces about one-third of the aqueous phase of the tear film and is normally situated within the anterior orbit, prolapses to emerge as a pink fleshy mass protruding over the edge of the third eyelid, between the third eyelid and the cornea. The condition usually develops during the first year of life and, while mild irritation may result, the condition is unsightly as much as anything else.

Corneal Disease

The cornea is the clear front part of the eye that provides the first step in the collection of light on its journey to be eventually focused onto the retina, and most corneal diseases will be manifested by alterations in corneal transparency. The cornea is an exquisitely innervated tissue, and defects in corneal integrity are accompanied by pain, which is demonstrated by squinting.

Corneal ulcers may occur secondary to trauma or to irritation from entropion or ectopic cilia. In middle-aged or older dogs, epithelial ulcerations may occur spontaneously due to an inherent defect; these are referred to as indolent or Boxer ulcers, in recognition of the breed in which we see the condition most frequently. Infection may occur secondarily. Ulcers can be potentially blinding conditions; severity is dependent upon the size and depth of the ulcer and other complicating features.

Non-ulcerative keratitis tends to have an immune-mediated component and is managed by topical immunosuppressants, usually corticosteroids. Corneal edema can occur in elderly dogs. It is due to a failure of the corneal endothelial 'pump.'

The cornea responds to chronic irritation by transforming

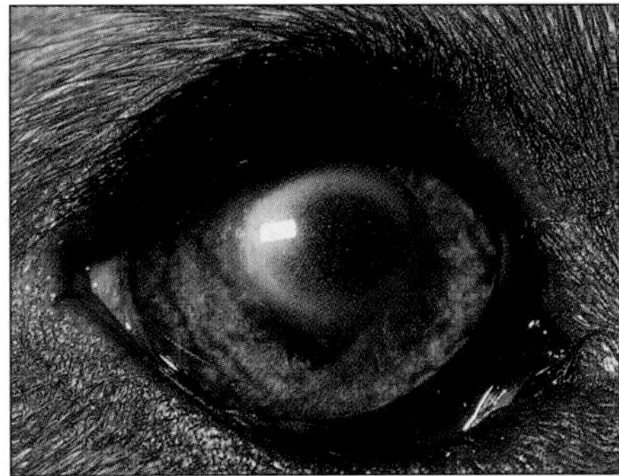

Lipid deposition can occur as a primary inherited dystrophy, or secondarily to hypercholesterolemia (in dogs frequently associated with hypothyroidism), chronic corneal inflammation or neoplasia. The deposits in this dog assume an oval pattern in the centre of the cornea.

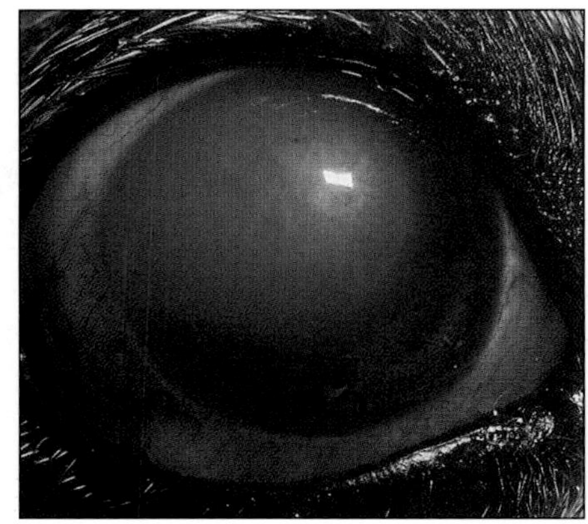

Corneal edema can develop as a slowly progressive process in elderly Boston Terriers, Miniature Dachshunds and Miniature Poodles, as well as others, as a result of the inability of the corneal endothelial 'pump' to maintain a state of dehydration.

into skin-like tissue that is evident clinically by pigmentation, scarring and vascularization; some cases may respond to tear stimulants, lubricants and topical corticosteroids, while others benefit from surgical narrowing of the eyelid opening in order to enhance corneal protection.

Uveitis

Inflammation of the vascular tissue of the eye–the uvea—is a common and potentially serious disease in dogs. While it may occur secondarily to trauma or other intraocular diseases, such as cataracts, most commonly uveitis is associated with some type of systemic infectious or neoplastic process. Uncontrolled, uveitis can lead to blinding cataracts, glaucoma and/or retinal detachments, and aggressive symptomatic therapy with dilating agents (to prevent pupillary adhesions) and anti-inflammatories are critical.

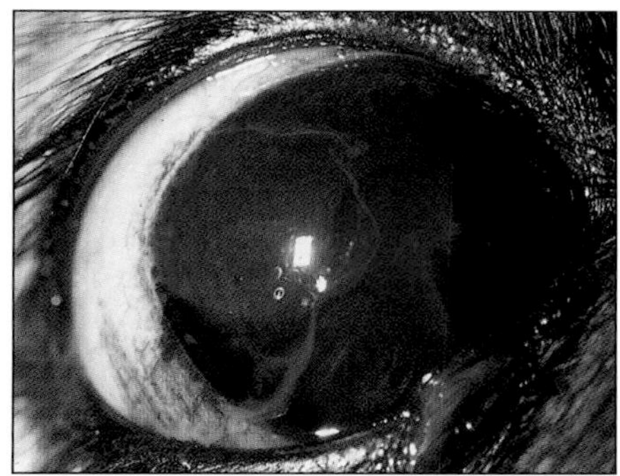

Medial pigmentary keratitis in this dog is associated with irritation from prominent facial folds.

Glaucoma

The eye is essentially a hollow fluid-filled sphere, and the pressure within is maintained by regulation of the rate of fluid production and fluid egress at 10–20 mms of mercury. The retinal cells are extremely sensitive to elevations of intraocular pressure and, unless controlled, permanent blindness can occur within hours to days. In acute glaucoma, the conjunctiva becomes congested, the cornea cloudy, the pupil moderate and fixed; the eye is generally painful and avisual. Increased constant signs of

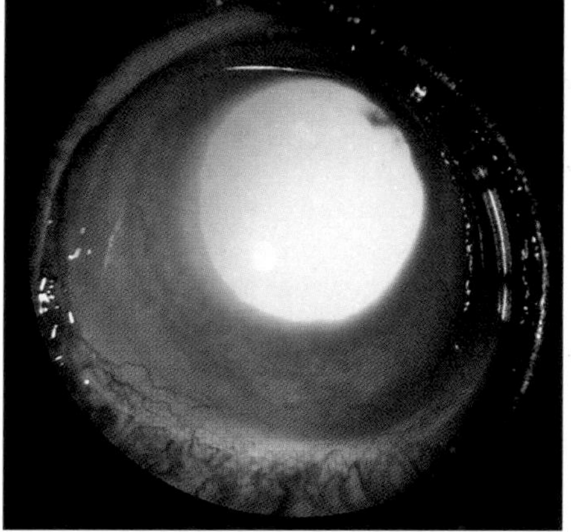

Glaucoma in the dog most commonly occurs as a sudden extreme elevation of intraocular pressure, frequently to three to four times the norm. The eye of this dog demonstrates the common signs of episcleral injection, or redness; mild diffuse corneal cloudiness, due to edema; and a mid-sized fixed pupil.

discomfort will accompany chronic cases.

Management of glaucoma is one of the most challenging situations the veterinary ophthalmologist faces; in spite of intense efforts, many of these cases will result in blindness.

Cataracts and Lens Dislocation

Cataracts are the most common blinding condition in dogs; fortunately, they are readily amenable to surgical intervention, with excellent results in terms of restoration of vision and replacement of the cataractous lens with a synthetic one. Most cataracts in dogs are inherited; less commonly cataracts can be secondary to trauma, other ocular diseases, including uveitis, glaucoma, lens luxation and retinal degeneration, or secondary to an underlying systemic metabolic disease, including diabetes and Cushing's disease. Signs include a progressive loss of the bright dark appearance of the pupil, which is replaced by a blue-grey hazy appearance. In this respect, cataracts need to be distinguished from the normal ageing process of nuclear sclerosis, which occurs in middle-aged or older animals, and has minimal effect on vision.

Lens dislocation occurs in dogs and frequently leads to secondary glaucoma; early removal of the dislocated lens is generally curative.

Retinal Disease

Retinal degenerations are usually inherited, but may be associated with vitamin E deficiency in dogs.

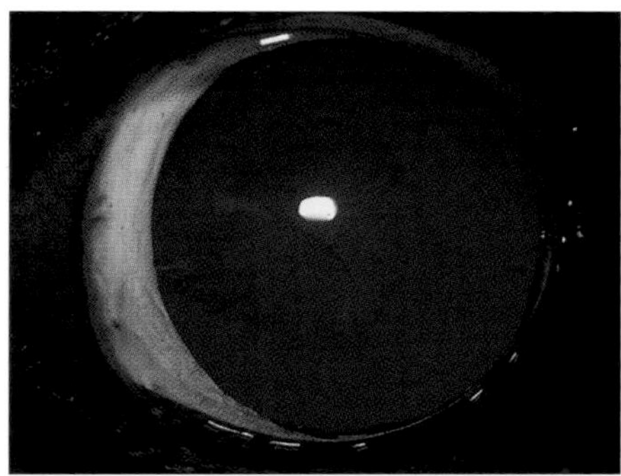

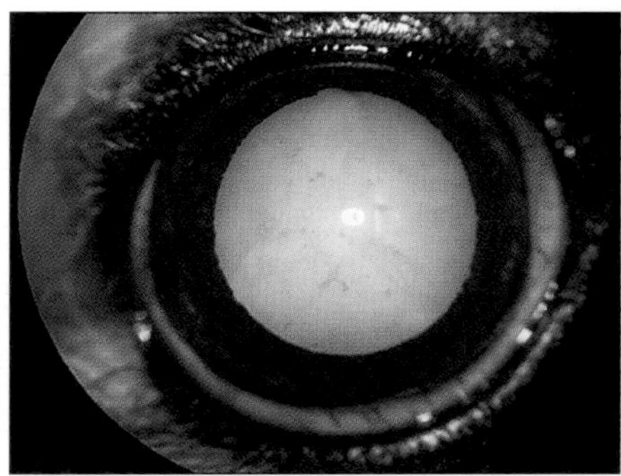

Left: The typical posterior subcapsular cataract appears between one and two years of age, but rarely progresses to where the animal has visual problems. Right: Inherited cataracts generally appear between three and six years of age, and progress to the stage seen where functional vision is significantly impaired.

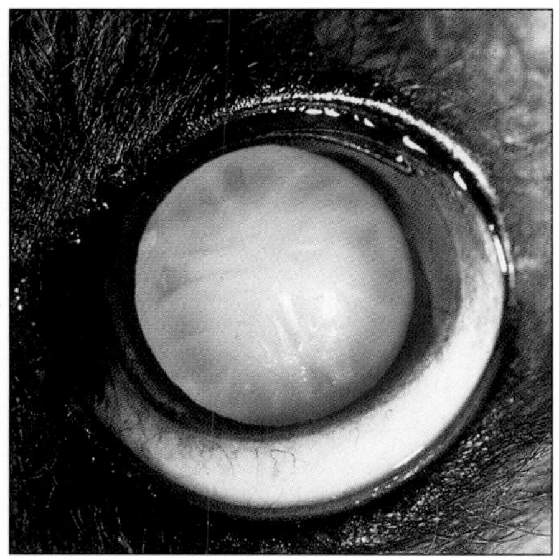

While signs are variable, most frequently one notes a decrease in vision over a period of months, which typically starts out as a night blindness. The cause of a more rapid loss of vision due to retinal degeneration occurs over days to weeks is labeled sudden acquired retinal degeneration or SARD; the outcome, however, is unfortunately usually similar to inherited and nutritional conditions, as the retinal tissues possess minimal regenerative capabilities. Most pets, however, with a bit of extra care and attention, show an amazing ability to adapt to an avisual world, and can be maintained as pets with a satisfactory quality of life. Detachment of the retina—due to accumulation of blood between the retina and the underling uvea, which is called the *choroid*—can occur secondarily to retinal tears or holes, tractional forces within the eye, or as a result of uveitis. These types of detachments may be amenable to surgical repair if diagnosed early.

Optic Nerve

Optic neuritis, or inflammation of the nerve that connects the eye with the brain stem, is a relatively uncommon condition that presents usually with rather sudden loss of vision and widely dilated non-responsive pupils.

Anterior lens luxation can occur as a primary disease in the terrier breeds, or secondarily to trauma. The fibres that hold the lens in place rupture and the lens may migrate through the pupil to be situated in front of the iris. Secondary glaucoma is a frequent and significant complication that can be avoided if the dislocated lens is removed surgically.

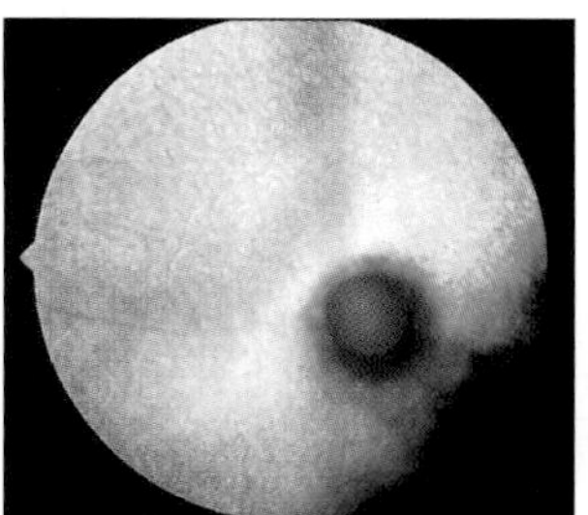

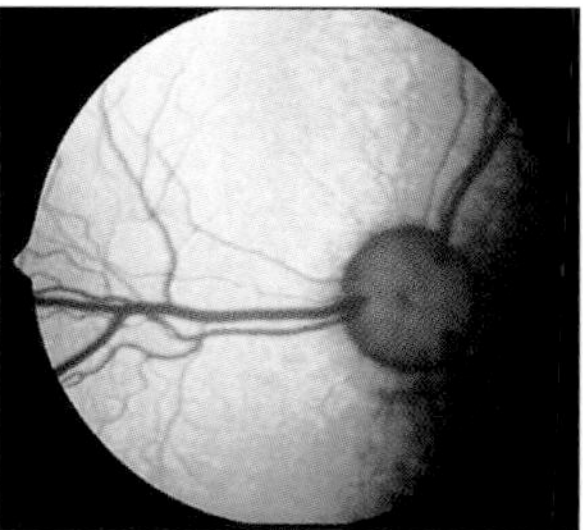

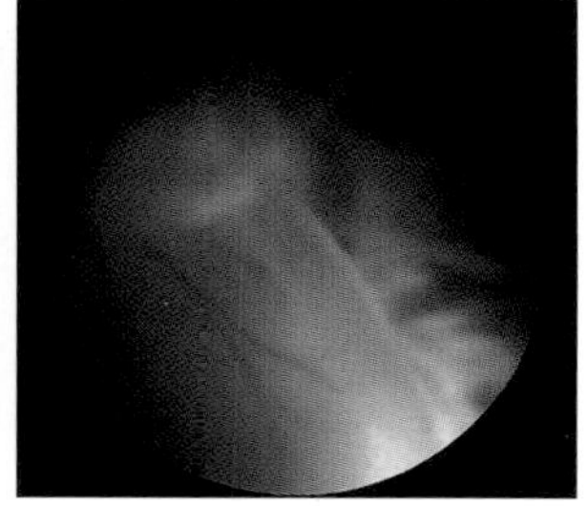

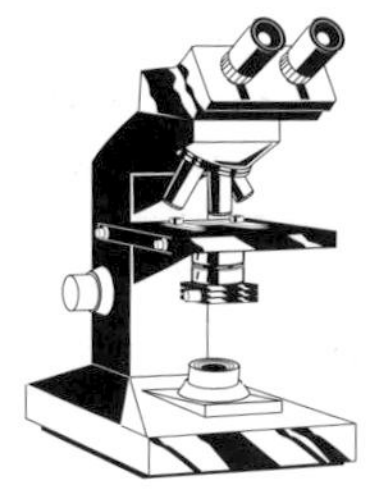

Left: The posterior pole of a normal fundus is shown; prominent are the head of the optic nerve and the retinal blood vessels. The retina is transparent, and the prominent green tapetum is seen superiorly.
Centre: An eye with inherited retinal dysplasia is depicted. The tapetal retina superior to the optic disc is disorganised, with multifocal areas of hyperplasia of the retinal pigment epithelium.
Right: Severe collie eye anomaly and a retinal detachment; this eye is unfortunately blind.

HOMEOPATHY:
an alternative to conventional medicine

'Less is Most'
Using this principle, the strength of a homeopathic remedy is measured by the number of serial dilutions that were undertaken to create it. The greater the number of serial dilutions, the greater the strength of the homeopathic remedy. The potency of a remedy that has been made by making a dilution of 1 part in 100 parts (or 1/100) is 1c or 1cH. If this remedy is subjected to a series of further dilutions, each one being 1/100, a more dilute and stronger remedy is produced. If the remedy is diluted in this way six times, it is called 6c or 6cH. A dilution of 6c is 1 part in 1000,000,000,000. In general, higher potencies in more frequent doses are better for acute symptoms and lower potencies in more infrequent doses are more useful for chronic, long-standing problems.

CURING OUR DOGS NATURALLY
Holistic medicine means treating the whole animal as a unique, perfect living being. Generally, holistic treatments do not suppress the symptoms that the body naturally produces, as do most medications prescribed by conventional doctors and vets. Holistic methods seek to cure disease by regaining balance and harmony in the patient's environment. Some of these methods include use of nutritional therapy, herbs, flower essences, aromatherapy, acupuncture, massage, chiropractic and, of course, the most popular holistic approach, homeopathy.
Homeopathy is a theory or system of treating illness with small doses of substances which, if administered in larger quantities, would produce the symptoms that the patient already has. This approach is often described as 'like cures like.' Although modern veterinary medicine is geared toward the 'quick fix,' homeopathy relies on the belief that, given the time, the body is able to heal itself and return to its natural, healthy state.

Choosing a remedy to cure a problem in our dogs is the difficult part of homeopathy. Consult with your veterinary surgeon for a professional diagnosis of your dog's symptoms. Often these symptoms require immediate conventional care. If your vet is willing, and somewhat knowledgeable, you may attempt a homeopathic remedy. Be aware that cortisone prevents homeopathic remedies from working. There are hundreds of possibilities and combinations to cure many problems in dogs, from basic physical problems such as excessive moulting, fleas or other parasites, unattractive doggy odour, bad breath, upset tummy, dry, oily or dull coat, diarrhoea, ear problems or eye discharge (including tears and dry or mucousy matter), to behavioural abnormalities, such as fear of loud noises, habitual licking, poor appetite, excessive barking, obesity and various phobias. From alumina to zincum metallicum, the remedies span the planet and the imagination…from flowers and weeds to chemicals, insect droppings, diesel smoke and volcanic ash.

Using 'Like to Treat Like'

Unlike conventional medicines that suppress symptoms, homeopathic remedies treat illnesses with small doses of substances that, if administered in larger quantities, would produce the symptoms that the patient already has. Whilst the same homeopathic remedy can be used to treat different symptoms in different dogs, here are some interesting remedies and their uses.

Apis Mellifica
(made from honey bee venom) can be used for allergies or to reduce swelling that occurs in acutely infected kidneys.

Diesel Smoke
can be used to help control travel sickness.

Calcarea Fluorica
(made from calcium fluoride which helps harden bone structure) can be useful in treating hard lumps in tissues.

Natrum Muriaticum
(made from common salt, sodium chloride) is useful in treating thin, thirsty dogs.

Nitricum Acidum
(made from nitric acid) is used for symptoms you would expect to see from contact with acids such as lesions, especially where the skin joins the linings of body orifices or openings such as the lips and nostrils.

Symphytum
(made from the herb knitbone, Symphytum officianale) is used to encourage bones to heal.

Urtica Urens
(made from the common stinging nettle) is used in treating painful, irritating rashes.

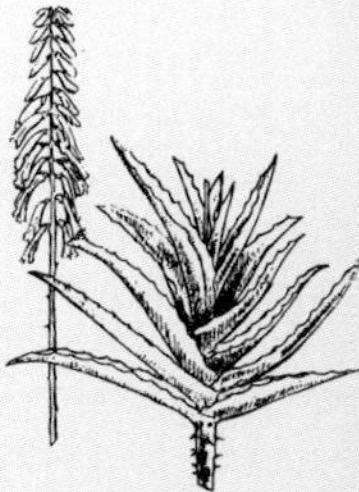

HOMEOPATHIC REMEDIES FOR YOUR DOG

Symptom/Ailment	Possible Remedy
ALLERGIES	Apis Mellifica 30c, Astacus Fluviatilis 6c, Pulsatilla 30c, Urtica Urens 6c
ALOPECIA	Alumina 30c, Lycopodium 30c, Sepia 30c, Thallium 6c
ANAL GLANDS (BLOCKED)	Hepar Sulphuris Calcareum 30c, Sanicula 6c, Silicea 6c
ARTHRITIS	Rhus Toxicodendron 6c, Bryonia Alba 6c
CATARACT	Calcarea Carbonica 6c, Conium Maculatum 6c, Phosphorus 30c, Silicea 30c
CONSTIPATION	Alumina 6c, Carbo Vegetabilis 30c, Graphites 6c, Nitricum Acidum 30c, Silicea 6c
COUGHING	Aconitum Napellus 6c, Belladonna 30c, Hyoscyamus Niger 30c, Phosphorus 30c
DIARRHOEA	Arsenicum Album 30c, Aconitum Napellus 6c, Chamomilla 30c, Mercurius Corrosivus 30c
DRY EYE	Zincum Metallicum 30c
EAR PROBLEMS	Aconitum Napellus 30c, Belladonna 30c, Hepar Sulphuris 30c, Tellurium 30c, Psorinum 200c
EYE PROBLEMS	Borax 6c, Aconitum Napellus 30c, Graphites 6c, Staphysagria 6c, Thuja Occidentalis 30c
GLAUCOMA	Aconitum Napellus 30c, Apis Mellifica 6c, Phosphorus 30c
HEAT STROKE	Belladonna 30c, Gelsemium Sempervirens 30c, Sulphur 30c
HICCOUGHS	Cinchona Deficinalis 6c
HIP DYSPLASIA	Colocynthis 6c, Rhus Toxicodendron 6c, Bryonia Alba 6c
INCONTINENCE	Argentum Nitricum 6c, Causticum 30c, Conium Maculatum 30c, Pulsatilla 30c, Sepia 30c
INSECT BITES	Apis Mellifica 30c, Cantharis 30c, Hypericum Perforatum 6c, Urtica Urens 30c
ITCHING	Alumina 30c, Arsenicum Album 30c, Carbo Vegetabilis 30c, Hypericum Perforatum 6c, Mezerium 6c, Sulphur 30c
KENNEL COUGH	Drosera 6c, Ipecacuanha 30c
MASTITIS	Apis Mellifica 30c, Belladonna 30c, Urtica Urens 1m
PATELLAR LUXATION	Gelsemium Sempervirens 6c, Rhus Toxicodendron 6c
PENIS PROBLEMS	Aconitum Napellus 30c, Hepar Sulphuris Calcareum 30c, Pulsatilla 30c, Thuja Occidentalis 6c
PUPPY TEETHING	Calcarea Carbonica 6c, Chamomilla 6c, Phytolacca 6c
TRAVEL SICKNESS	Cocculus 6c, Petroleum 6c

Recognising a Sick Dog

Unlike colicky babies and cranky children, our canine kids cannot tell us when they are feeling ill. Therefore, there are a number of signs that owners can identify to know that their dogs are not feeling well.

Take note for physical manifestations such as:

- unusual, bad odour, including bad breath
- excessive moulting
- wax in the ears, chronic ear irritation
- oily, flaky, dull haircoat
- mucous, tearing or similar discharge in the eyes
- fleas or mites
- mucous in stool, diarrhoea
- sensitivity to petting or handling
- licking at paws, scratching face, etc.

Keep an eye out for behavioural changes as well including:

- lethargy, idleness
- lack of patience or general irritability
- lack of appetite, digestive problems
- phobias (fear of people, loud noises, etc.)
- strange behaviour, suspicion, fear
- coprophagia
- more frequent barking
- whimpering, crying

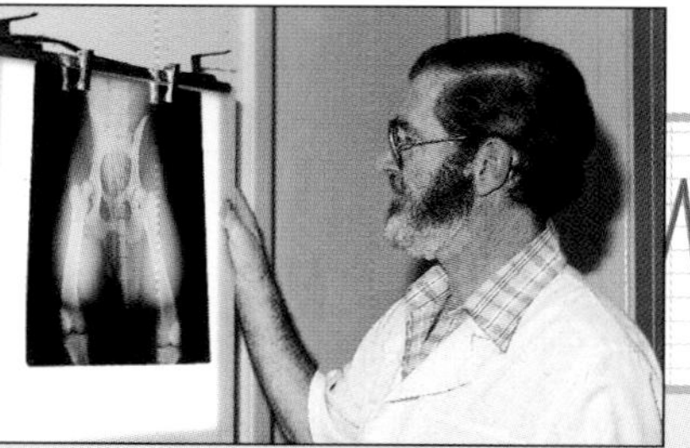

Get Well Soon

You don't need a DVR or a BVMA to provide good TLC to your sick or recovering dog, but you do need to pay attention to some details that normally wouldn't bother him. The following tips will aid Fido's recovery and get him back on his paws again:

- Keep his space free of irritating smells, like heavy perfumes and air fresheners.
- Rest is the best medicine! Avoid harsh lighting that will prevent your dog from sleeping. Shade him from bright sunlight during the day and dim the lights in the evening.
- Keep the noise level down. Animals are more sensitive to sound when they are sick.
- Be attentive to any necessary temperature adjustments. A dog with a fever needs a cool room and cold liquids. A bitch that is whelping or recovering from surgery will be more comfortable in a warm room, consuming warm liquids and food.
- You wouldn't send a sick child back to school early, so don't rush your dog back into a full routine until he seems absolutely ready.

The Clumber Spaniel's calm, noble demeanour makes him a biddable show dog. Though lacking the exuberance and showmanship of an Afghan Hound or Poodle in the ring, Clumbers always exude intelligence and dignity.

SHOWING YOUR CLUMBER SPANIEL

When you purchased your Clumber Spaniel, you will have made it clear to the breeder whether you wanted one just as a loveable companion and pet, or if you hoped to be buying a Clumber Spaniel with show prospects. No reputable breeder will have sold you a young puppy saying that it was definitely of show quality for so much can go wrong during the early weeks and months of a puppy's development. If you plan to show, what you will hopefully have acquired is a puppy with 'show potential.'

To the novice, exhibiting a Clumber Spaniel in the show ring may look easy but it usually takes a lot of hard work and devotion to do top winning at a show such as the prestigious Crufts, not to mention a little luck too!

The first concept that the canine novice learns when watching a dog show is that each dog first competes against members of its own breed. Once the judge has selected the best member of each breed, provided that the show is judged on a Group system, that chosen dog will compete with other dogs in its group. Finally the best of each group will compete for Best in Show and Reserve Best in Show.

Conformation showing requires a well-trained Clumber Spaniel that nearly resembles the dog described in the breed standard. The judge compares each dog to the breed standard.

The second concept that you must understand is that the dogs are not actually competing against one another. The judge compares each dog against the breed standard, which is a written description of the ideal specimen of the breed. Whilst some early breed standards were indeed based on specific dogs that were famous or popular, many dedicated enthusiasts say that a perfect specimen, described in the standard, has never been bred. Thus the 'perfect' dog has never walked into a show ring, has never been bred and, to the woe of dog breeders around the globe, does not exist. Breeders attempt to get as close to this ideal as possible, with every litter, but theoretically the 'perfect' dog is so elusive that it is impossible. (And if the 'perfect' dog were born, breeders and judges would never agree that it was indeed 'perfect.')

If you are interested in exploring dog shows, your best bet is to join your local all-breed club, national parent club or, in the case of less rare breeds than Clumbers, your local breed club. These clubs often host both Championship and Open Shows, and sometimes Match meetings and Special Events, all of which could be of interest, even if you are only an onlooker. Clubs also send out newsletters and some organise training days and seminars in order that people may learn more about their chosen breed. To locate the nearest club for you, contact The Kennel Club, the ruling body for the British dog world. The Kennel Club governs not only conformation shows but also working trials, obedience trials, agility trials and field trials. The Kennel Club furnishes the rules and regulations for all these events plus general dog registration and other basic requirements of dog ownership. Its annual show called the Crufts Dog Show, held in Birmingham, is the largest benched show in England. Every year around 20,000 of the UK's best dogs qualify to participate in this marvellous show which lasts four days.

The Kennel Club governs many different kinds of shows in Great Britain, Australia, South Africa and beyond. At the most competitive and prestigious of these shows, the Championship Shows, a dog can earn Challenge Certificates (CCs), and thereby become a Show Champion or a

DID YOU KNOW?

You can get information about dog shows from kennel clubs and breed clubs:

Fédération Cynologique Internationale
14, rue Leopold II, B-6530 Thuin, Belgium
www.fci.be

The Kennel Club
1-5 Clarges St., Piccadilly
London W1Y 8AB, UK
www.the-kennel-club.org.uk

American Kennel Club
5580 Centerview Drive
Raleigh, NC 27606-3390, USA
www.akc.org

Canadian Kennel Club
89 Skyway Ave., Suite 100
Etobicoke, Ontario
M9W 6R4 Canada
www.ckc.ca

This proud owner has handled her Clumber Spaniel puppy to 'Best Puppy in Show' at the National Gundog Association. What a promising career this duo has to look forward to!

Champion. A dog must earn three Challenge Certificates under three different judges to earn the prefix of 'Sh Ch' or 'Ch.' Note that some breeds must also qualify in a field trial in order to gain the title of full champion. Challenge Certificates are awarded to a very small percentage of the dogs competing, especially as dogs which are already Champions compete with others for these coveted CCs. The number of Challenge Certificates awarded in any one year is based upon the total number of dogs in each breed entered for competition. There are three types of Championship Shows: an all-breed General Championship Show for all Kennel Club recognised breeds, a Group Championship Show, limited to breeds within one of the groups, and a Breed Show, usually

DID YOU KNOW?

Just like with anything else, there is a certain etiquette to the show ring that can only be learned through experience. Showing your dog can be quite intimidating to you as a novice when it seems as if everyone else knows what they are

doing. You can familiarise yourself with ring procedure beforehand by taking a class to prepare you and your dog for conformation showing or by talking with an experienced handler. When you are in the ring, listen and pay attention to the judge and follow his/her directions. Remember, even the most skilled handlers had to start somewhere. Keep it up and you too will become a proficient handler before too long!

confined to a single breed. The Kennel Club determines which breeds at which Championship Shows will have the opportunity to earn Challenge Certificates (or tickets). Serious exhibitors often will opt not to participate if the tickets are withheld at a particular show. This policy makes earning championships even more difficult to accomplish.

Open Shows are generally less competitive and are frequently used as 'practice shows' for young dogs. There are hundreds of Open Shows each year that can be invitingly social events and are great first show experiences for the novice. Even if you're considering just watching a show to wet your paws, an Open Show is a great choice.

Whilst Championship and Open Shows are most important for the beginner to understand, there are other types of shows in which the interested dog owner can participate. Training clubs sponsor Matches that can be entered on the day of the show for a nominal fee. In these introductory-level exhibitions, two dogs are pulled out of a hat and 'matched,' the winner of that match goes on to the next round, and eventually only one dog is left undefeated.

Exemption Shows are much more light-hearted affairs with usually only four pedigree classes and several 'fun' classes, all of which can be entered on the day. The proceeds of an Exemption Show must be given to a charity. These shows are sometimes held in conjunction with small agricultural shows. Limited Shows are also available in small numbers, but entry is restricted to members of the club which hosts the show, although one can usually join the club when making an entry.

Before you actually step into the ring, you would be well advised to sit back and observe the judge's ring procedure. If it is your first time in the ring, do not be over-anxious and run to the front of the line. It is much better to stand back and study how the exhibitor in front of you is performing. The judge asks each handler to 'stand' the dog, hopefully showing the dog off to his best advantage. The judge will observe the dog from a distance and from different angles, approach the dog, check his teeth, overall structure, alertness and muscle tone, as well as consider how well the dog 'conforms' to the standard. Most importantly, the judge will have the exhibitor move the dog around the ring in some pattern that he or she should specify (another advantage to not going first, but always listen since some judges change their directions, and the judge is always right!) Finally the judge will give the dog one last look before moving on to the next exhibitor.

If you are not in the top three at your first show, do not be discouraged. Be patient and consistent and you may eventually find yourself in the winning line-up. Remember that the winners were once in your shoes and have devoted many hours and much money to earn the placement. If you find that your dog is losing every time and never getting a nod, it may be time to consider a different dog sport or just enjoy your Clumber Spaniel as a pet.

To compete in obedience or working trials, the Clumber Spaniel must be able to follow the handler's commands without fail. Note how attentive this Clumber is to his master's next command.

WORKING TRIALS

Working trials can be entered by any well-trained dog of any breed, not just Gundogs or Working dogs. Many dogs that earn The Kennel Club Good Citizen Dog award choose to participate in a working trial. There are five stakes at both open and championship levels: Companion Dog (CD), Utility Dog (UD), Working Dog (WD), Tracking Dog (TD) and Patrol Dog (PD). As in conformation shows, dogs compete against a standard and if the dog reaches the qualifying mark, it obtains a certificate. Divided into groups, each exercise must be achieved 70 percent in order to qualify. If the dog achieves 80 percent in the open level, it receives a Certificate of Merit (COM); in the championship level, it receives a Qualifying Certificate. At the CD stake, dogs must participate in four groups: Control, Stay, Agility and Search (Retrieve and Nosework). At the next three levels, UD, WD and TD, there are only three groups: Control, Agility and Nosework.

This marvelously trained Clumber Spaniel is clearing the bar jump at an obedience trial.

Agility consists of three jumps: a vertical scale up a six-foot wall of planks; a clear jump over a basic three-foot hurdle with a removable top bar; and a long jump across angled planks stretching nine feet.

To earn the UD, WD and TD, dogs must track approximately one-half mile for articles laid from one-half hour to three hours ago. Tracks consist of turns and legs, and fresh ground is used for each participant. Clumbers enjoy working for a Tracking degree and are quite good at it.

The fifth stake, PD, involves teaching manwork, which is not recommended for every breed.

FIELD TRIALS AND WORKING TESTS

Working tests are frequently used to prepare dogs for field trials, the purpose of which is to heighten the instincts and natural abilities of Gundogs. Live game is not used in working tests. Unlike field trials, working tests do not count toward a dog's record at The Kennel Club, though the same judges often oversee working tests. Field trials began in England in 1947 and are only moderately popular amongst dog folk. Whilst breeders of Working and Gundog breeds concern themselves with the field abilities of their dogs, there is considerably less interest in field trials than dog shows. In order

Here's Am and Can Ch Critter's Hungry Heart, TD, CGC, showing off his remarkable nose. Clumbers make fine tracking dogs and prove consistent, persistent performers.

for dogs to become full champions, certain breeds must qualify in the field as well. Upon gaining three CCs in the show ring, the dog is designated a Show Champion (Sh Ch). The title Champion (Ch) requires that the dog gain an award at a field trial, be a 'special qualifier' at a field trial or pass a 'special show dog qualifier' judged by a field trial judge on a shooting day.

AGILITY TRIALS

Agility trials began in the United Kingdom in 1977 and have since spread around the world, especially to the United States, where they enjoy strong popularity. The handler directs his dog over an obstacle course that includes jumps (such as those used in the working trials), as well as tyres, the dog walk, weave poles, pipe tunnels, collapsed tunnels, etc. The Kennel Club requires that dogs not be trained for agility until they are 12 months old. This dog sport proves to be great fun for dog and owner and interested owners should join a training club that has obstacles and experienced agility handlers who can introduce you and your dog to the 'ropes' (and tyres, tunnels and so on).

FÉDÉRATION CYNOLOGIQUE INTERNATIONALE

Established in 1911, the Fédération Cynologique Internationale (FCI) represents the 'world kennel club.' This international body brings uniformity to the breeding, judging and showing of pure-bred dogs. Although the FCI originally included only five European nations: France,

Opposite page: A first for the Clumber Spaniel in the USA: this is Am Ch Clussex's Country Sunrise, winning the most prestigious show in the USA, the Westminster Kennel Club in 1996. Brady, as he was known, was handled by Lisa Jane Alston-Myers, winning under judge D Roy Holloway.

DID YOU KNOW?

The FCI *does not* issue pedigrees. The FCI members and contract partners are responsible for issuing pedigrees and training judges in their own countries. The FCI does maintain a list of judges and makes sure that they are recognised throughout the FCI member countries.

The FCI also *does not* act as a breeder referral; breeder information is available from FCI-recognised national canine societies in each of the FCI's member countries.

Holland, Germany, Austria and Belgium (which remains its headquarters), the organisation today embraces nations on six continents and recognises well over 300 breeds of pure-bred dog. There are three titles attainable through the FCI: the International Champion, which is the most prestigious; the International Beauty Champion, which is based on aptitude certificates in different countries; and the International Trial Champion, which is based on achievement in obedience trials in different countries. Dogs and handlers from around the globe can participate in these impressive FCI spectacles, the largest of which is the World Dog Show, hosted in a different country each year. FCI sponsors both national and international shows. The hosting country determines the judging system and breed standards are always based on the breed's country of origin.

Gait is evaluated by the judge. The Clumber should move with effortless drive in its characteristic rolling fashion.

BEST IN SHOW
THE WESTMINSTER KENNEL CLUB

GLOSSARY

This glossary is intended to help you, the Clumber Spaniel owner, better understand the specific terms used in this book as well as other terms that might surface in discussions with your veterinary surgeon during his care of your Clumber Spaniel.

Abscess a pus-filled inflamed area of body tissue.

Acral lick granuloma unexplained licking of an area, usually the leg, that prevents healing of original wound.

Acute disease a disease whose onset is sudden and fast.

Albino an animal totally lacking in pigment (always white).

Allergy a known sensitivity that results from exposure to a given allergen.

Alopecia lack of hair.

Amaurosis an unexplained blindness from the retina.

Anaemia red-blood-cell deficiency.

Arthritis joint inflammation.

Atopic dermatitis congenital-allergen-caused inflammation of the skin.

Atrophy wasting away caused by faulty nutrition; a reduction in size.

Bloat gastric dilatation.

Calculi mineral 'stone' located in a vital organ, i.e. gall bladder.

Cancer a tumour that continues to expand and grow rapidly.

Carcinoma cancerous growth in the skin.

Cardiac arrhythmia irregular heartbeat.

Cardiomyopathy heart condition involving the septum and flow of blood.

Cartilage strong but pliable body tissue.

Cataract clouding of the eye lens.

Cherry eye third eyelid prolapsed gland.

Cleft palate improper growth of the two hard palates of the mouth.

Collie eye anomaly congenital defect of the back of the eye.

Congenital not the same as hereditary, but present at birth.

Congestive heart failure fluid buildup in lungs due to heart's inability to pump.

Conjunctivitis inflammation of the membrane that lines eyelids and eyeball.

Cow hocks poor rear legs that point inward; always incorrect.

Cryptorchid male animal with only one or both testicles undescended.

Cushing's disease condition caused by adrenal gland producing too much corticosteroid.

Cyst uninflamed swelling contain non-pus-like fluid.

Degeneration deterioration of tissue.

Demodectic mange red-mite infestation caused by *Demodex canis.*

Dermatitis skin inflammation.

Dew claw a functionless digit found on the inside of a dog's leg.

Diabetes insipidus disease of the hypothalamus gland resulting in animal passing great amounts of diluted urine.

Diabetes mellitus excess of glucose in blood stream.

Distemper contagious viral disease of dogs that can be most deadly.

Distichiasis double layer of eyelashes on an eyelid.

Dysplasia abnormal, poor development of a body part, especially a joint.

Dystrophy inherited degeneration.

Eclampsia potentially deadly disease in post-partum bitches due to calcium deficiency.

Ectropion outward turning of the eyelid; opposite of entropion.

Eczema inflammatory skin disease, marked by itching.

Edema fluid accumulation in a specific area.

Entropion inward turning of the eyelid.

Epilepsy chronic disease of the nervous system characterised by seizures.

Exocrine pancreatic insufficiency body's inability to produce enough enzymes to aid digestion.

False pregnancy pseudo-pregnancy, bitch shows all signs of pregnancy but there is no fertilization.

Follicular mange demodectic mange.

Gastric dilatation bloat caused by the dog's swallowing air resulting in distended, twisted stomach.

Gastroenteritis stomach or intestinal inflammation.

Gingivitis gum inflammation caused by plaque buildup.

Glaucoma increased eye pressure affecting vision.

Haematemesis vomiting blood.

Haematoma blood-filled swollen area.

Haematuria blood in urine.

Haemophilia bleeding disorder due to lack of clotting factor.

Haemorrhage bleeding.

Heat stroke condition due to over-heating of an animal.

Heritable an inherited condition.

Hot spot moist eczema characterised by dog's licking in same area.

Hyperglycemia excess glucose in blood.

Hypersensitivity allergy.

Hypertrophic cardiomyopathy left-ventricle septum becomes thickened and obstructs blood flow to heart.

Hypertrophic osteodystrophy condition affecting normal bone development.

Hypothyroidism disease caused by insufficient thyroid hormone.

Hypertrophy increased cell size resulting in enlargement of organ.

Hypoglycemia glucose deficiency in blood.

Idiopathic disease of unknown cause.

IgA deficiency immunoglobin deficiency resulting in digestive, breathing and skin problems.

Inbreeding mating two closely related animals, eg, mother—son.

Inflammation the changes that occur to a tissue after injury, characterised by swelling, redness, pain, etc.

Jaundice yellow coloration of mucous membranes.

Keratoconjunctivitis sicca dry eye.

Leukaemia malignant disease characterised by white blood cells released into blood stream.

Lick granuloma excessive licking of a wound, preventing proper healing.

Merle coat colour that is diluted.

Monorchid a male animal with only one testicle descended.

Neuritis nerve inflammation.

Nicitating membrane third eyelid pulling across the eye.

Nodular dermatofibrosis lumps on toes and legs, usually associated with cancer of kidney and uterus.

Osteochondritis bone or cartilage inflammation.

Outcrossing mating two breed representatives from different families.

Pancreatitis pancreas inflammation.

Pannus chronic superficial keratitis, affecting pigment and blood vessels of cornea.

Panosteitis inflammation of leg bones, characterised by lameness.

Papilloma wart.

Patellar luxation slipped kneecap, common in small dogs.

Patent ductus arteriosus an open blood vessel between pulmonary artery and aorta.

Penetrance frequency in which a trait shows up in offspring of animals carrying that inheritable trait.

Periodontitis acute or chronic inflammation of tissue surround the tooth.

Pneumonia lung inflammation.

Progressive retinal atrophy congenital disease of retina causing blindness.

Pruritis persistent itching.

Retinal atrophy thin retina.

Seborrhea dry scurf or excess oil deposits on the skin.

Stomatitis mouth inflammation.

Tumour solid or fluid-filled swelling resulting from abnormal growth.

Uremia waste product buildup in blood due to disease of kidneys.

Uveitis inflammation of the iris.

Von Willebrand's disease hereditary bleeding disease.

Wall eye lack of colour in the iris.

Weaning separating the mother from her dependent, nursing young.

Zoonosis animal disease communicable to humans.

INDEX

*Page numbers in **boldface** indicate illustrations.*

My Clumber Spaniel

PUT YOUR PUPPY'S FIRST PICTURE HERE

Dog's Name ______________________________

Date ______________ Photographer ______________________